# LITTLE MIRACLES OF KATRINA

# LITTLE MIRACLES OF KATRINA

*by*

M.V. Despenza

Copyright © 2025 by M.V. Despenza

All rights reserved. No part of this publication may be reproduced, distributed, or transmitted in any form or by any means, including photocopying, recording, or other electronic or mechanical methods, without the prior written permission of the publisher, except in the case of brief quotations embodied in critical reviews or certain other noncommercial uses permitted by copyright law. For permission requests, write to the publisher at the address below:

**Books by M.V. Despenza, LLC**
Mandeville, Louisiana
www.BooksbyMVDespenza.com

ISBN (Paperback): 979-8-9933150-0-3
ISBN (Hardcover): 979-8-9933150-1-0
ISBN (Digital PDF): 979-8-9933150-5-8
ISBN (eBook EPUB): 979-8-9933150-2-7
ISBN (Audiobook): 979-8-9933150-9-6

Library of Congress Control Number: 2025921337

U.S. Copyright Office Registration Number: 1-15010180591


First Edition 2025

Printed in the United States of America

# Dedication

Hurricane Katrina was the most devastating event to hit the New Orleans area in my lifetime. Those of us who personally experienced the storm's fury, whether directly or indirectly, still feel the emotional impact twenty years later. We have repaired, rebuilt, revived, restored, relocated, regenerated, recuperated, refreshed, recommitted, and re-established. However, we have not entirely recovered, and I am unsure if we ever will. In certain areas, scores of new and impressive structures stand, while in others, it feels as if Katrina struck just yesterday. There are still sights and smells of this deadly natural force, and these reminders will stay with us for the rest of our lives. For these reasons, I dedicate this book to everyone affected by Katrina, especially the residents of New Orleans on the morning of Monday, August 29, 2005. We will forever bear the psychological scars of this powerful natural disaster. This is a shared experience, though a very sorrowful one, that continues to connect us. I pray for you, your families, and your loved ones. God bless you all!

I want to thank everyone who played a part in my journey and the little miracles captured in this book: my husband, Lamart Joseph Buggage; my sister, Vicki Despenza Carriere; my cousins, Monica Johnson, Angela Johnson, Cordell Johnson, Geraldine Levy, and her family; Arthur and Bernadine Moran (in absentia); my mother-in-law, Erma Sherman Buggage (in absentia); and my precious, precious Black Cat. We created these little miracles together! A final shout-out to my three precious kitties: Simba,

Stella Bella, and Vanilla Bean. They surprisingly managed to find their way into my writing room during the many months I worked on my book, as I searched for the right words to tell my story. By stepping into an imaginary time capsule to relive the events of 2005, the emotions that resurfaced evoked a range of new feelings. Yet, with a slight tilt of my head, I was inexplicably grounded as I watched my little fur babies curled up in their favorite sleep spots, reassuring Mommy that, after all the pain and despair of Hurricane Katrina, by God's grace and blessings, I had indeed survived and "lived to tell the story," as they say.

# Table of Contents

Introduction .................................................................. iii
NOLA Dictionary ........................................................... ix
1 The Big Easy ............................................................... 1
2 Life in the Crescent City Pre-Katrina ........................... 5
3 Get Ready, Here She Comes ........................................ 9
4 The Shelters of Last Resort and Lost Hope ................ 19
5 The Morans' Unconventional Rescue ......................... 31
6 The Detour to the Family Reunion ............................ 53
7 My Promise to Black Cat ........................................... 77
8 Miss Erma's Planted Message ................................... 101
9 It's Waiting for You ................................................... 117
10 She Touched Two Sisters ......................................... 131
11 One Last Miracle ..................................................... 141
12 The Why for This Book .......................................... 155
Bibliography ................................................................ 161
Acknowledgements ..................................................... 167
About the Author ........................................................ 171

# Introduction

How do you define miracles? For people of faith, are they only the miraculous events that Jesus Christ performed during His thirty-three years on this earth? Events such as raising Lazarus from the dead or turning water into wine at the wedding at Cana? And are all miracles topped by the greatest miracle of all, the resurrection? For those who are not faith-based, is a miracle simply something that occurred but should not have happened by normal means? In either case, we experience these phenomena regularly and sometimes fail to recognize how frequently they occur.

The Merriam-Webster online dictionary defines a miracle as "an extraordinary event manifesting divine intervention in human affairs, or an extremely outstanding or unusual event, thing, or accomplishment." In today's world, we often think of miracles as these grand occurrences that attract extensive news coverage and amazement, because what was once unthinkable has now become not only possible but also achievable.

Consider Captain Chesley "Sully" Sullenberger's incredible emergency landing of a 150-passenger airplane on the Hudson River on January 15, 2009. Who could have guessed that Flight 1549, which took off from LaGuardia Airport headed for Charlotte, North Carolina, would hit a flock of geese at 3,000 feet, lose both engines, and descend at a rate of 1,000 feet per minute? There wasn't enough time for Captain Sullenberger to return to LaGuardia, so he calmly informed the air traffic controller and his co-pilot, Jeffrey Skiles, that he planned to land the Airbus A320 onto, not into, the Hudson River.

In shock, horror, and disbelief, the controller, Patrick Harten, responded with, "I'm sorry, say again?" He thought the plane was about to catastrophically crash into the river. He believed neither the passengers nor the crew members would ever survive an attempt to land in the river. And yet, they did. New York Governor David Paterson declared that day, "I believe that we've had a miracle on the Hudson."

And do you remember the Chilean Mining Accident in 2012, where thirty-three coal miners were trapped in the San Jose Copper Mine in northern Chile for sixty-nine days? Despite having virtually no food or water while their rescue took longer than expected, they all survived. The miners' chances of survival under those conditions were estimated to be less than two percent, but they clearly defied the odds.

Finally, there's the incredible story of four innocent children who survived a plane crash in the Amazon, where the pilot, a second passenger, and the children's mother were all killed. Remarkably, all four children survived in the jungle for forty days. The determined thirteen-year-old daughter managed to save her nine-year-old and four-year-old brothers, as well as her eleven-month-old baby sister. The odds that anyone, especially young children, could have survived in such a dense jungle full of predators are nothing short of miraculous.

We hear these stories and immediately accept them as miracles. But what about the small, everyday miracles that are meaningful to only a few people? Or maybe just one person? Small miracles that don't make the six o'clock news but are just as captivating or wondrous. I call these little miracles. We experience these moments every day, and I'm not sure we even realize it. Have you ever heard of a terrible car accident where everyone walks away alive with only minor scratches and bruises? You can't explain how it happened; you're just glad it did. But deep down, you believe or at least acknowledge that it was an extraordinary and unexpected event. Think about the times you've said, "Oh my God!" when you've heard someone survived a crash, a fire, or a fall from a roof that they shouldn't have lived through.

I have experienced many small miracles over the decades, and since then, I have always noticed these wonderful, tiny moments that have blessed my life. So, it's no surprise that this book is called Little Miracles of Katrina. The events I experienced in the days and weeks after Hurricane Katrina were nothing short of small miracles; moments that would make the average person, whether they have faith or not, ask, "How did that happen?" Non-believers would probably say that each was a coincidence, luck, karma, a sign from the universe, or just a fluke. These are all reasonable ideas, but my heart and faith see these events as something more.

These were God-given experiences that allowed me to help others and myself. Situations that, each on its own, could be seen as a coincidence or twist of fate. But together? I'm not so sure. I believe these were small miracles. Period. Understand that I, by no means, feel as though God chose me for these moments, as I am nobody special. I did not receive an extra dose of heavenly blessing. I think anyone who volunteered to take on some of these tasks would have had the same outcome. It just happened to be me.

I wrote this book to capture the small miracles that carried my family and me through the days and weeks after Hurricane Katrina in the summer of 2005. I never kept a journal of these events. I experienced them firsthand and later shared them with family and friends, often bringing both laughter and tears. It was their reactions, the way these stories touched them, that motivated me to share them with you.

Although I share experiences that I believe are God's will, my aim is not to convert anyone into a person of faith or to challenge the beliefs of any religious group that does not believe in miracles. I wrote this book to show that, even when life feels disheartening, at any moment and on any day, we might encounter an event that restores the hope we thought was gone. When pessimism dominates, hope steps in with strength.

I ask you to read this book with an open mind and heart. If, by turning these pages, I can give hope to even one person and touch their heart, then the time and effort I have invested in journaling my experiences will have been worthwhile. I genuinely hope that person is you.

# NOLA Dictionary

*Before we begin, I would be remiss if I didn't share a few NOLA terms with you. We've got a language and rhythm all our own, shaped by history, culture, and community. Some words may not show up in Webster's, but I promise you, they're real, and they're ours.*

**NOLA:** New Orleans, Louisiana (the one and only)

**The Big Easy:** That's what folks like to call New Orleans, and for good reason. Life down here just moves at a different pace. Nobody's in too much of a hurry, and if they are, they probably aren't from here. Some say it stuck because of our laid-back vibe, good food, good music, and plenty of laughter. Others say it came about when people compared us to New York, "The Big Apple." Up there, it's hustle. Down here, it's ease. Porch swings, bread pudding, second lines, and the kind of joy that lets you get there when you get there.

*And speaking of Second Lines…*

**Second Line:** A second line is a parade, but not the kind where you catch beads; it's the kind where you catch the rhythm. It's joy in motion, the heartbeat of the city. Neighbors, friends, and strangers fall into step together, dancing, waving handkerchiefs, and sporting umbrellas as they follow the music through the streets. If you see a second line in progress, put your inhibitions aside, grab a hankie, scarf, paper towel, napkin, whatever, and jump in. This is how we party in New Orleans: catching beads, catching joy, and most of all, catching rhythm.

**Crescent City**: One of New Orleans' many nicknames, born from the natural bend of the Mississippi River that curves around the city like a crescent. Locals use it with pride. *"I was born and raised in the Crescent City."* It's not just geography, it's identity.

**Crescent City Connection:** The "CCC" is the bridge that links the east and west banks of the river. New Orleans and the French Quarter sit on the East Bank; Algiers, Gretna, Harvey, Marrero, and Westwego are on the West Bank. When I was growing up, it was just the Mississippi River Bridge. Some folks still call it that — old habits die hard in the Big Easy.

**Parish**: In Louisiana, we don't have counties; we have parishes, a legacy of our Catholic heritage. Orleans Parish, Jefferson Parish, et al, same as counties elsewhere. Even our correctional facility is still called "Parish Prison."

**Levee:** In New Orleans, a levee isn't just a mound of dirt; it's our lifeline. These man-made walls of earth and concrete keep the Mississippi River and Lake Pontchartrain from swallowing our neighborhoods. We walk our dogs on them, jog on them, ride bikes on them, snap pictures on them, and sometimes take a spill on them (as you'll see in Chapter 5). But when a hurricane comes, we pray they hold. If they fail, water doesn't trickle in; it roars through like a broken dam.

**The Bowl:** When folks say New Orleans is shaped like a bowl, they're not exaggerating. Much of the city sits below sea level, cradled between Lake Pontchartrain to the north and the Mississippi River to the south. The river's natural levees are "high ground," but everything slopes down from there, like the bottom of a bowl. That's why flooding has always been one of our greatest vulnerabilities.

**Below Sea Level:** In NOLA, "below sea level" means parts of the city actually sit lower than the nearby lake and river. Both stand higher than our neighborhoods, so we rely on levees and pumps to keep water out. When those fail, the city fills fast. Heavy rains or storm surges flow right into the low spots — and unless the pumps and canals work overtime, the water stays.

**Neutral Ground:** The name goes back to early New Orleans, when the French and Americans would meet along Canal Street, each on their respective side of the street. Neutral territory. Everywhere else it's called a median, but here, it's neutral ground. And no, it's not where nutria roam free. It's where we set up ladders and tents for Mardi Gras, where we stand if the light changes too fast, and where folks park their cars during storms, crossing their fingers they don't come back to a flood... or worse, the boot. *(And if you're not from here, just know: "the boot" is that ugly clamp the city slaps on your tire before hauling your car away. One look at it and you know you're S.O.L.)*

# Chapter 1

## The Big Easy

New Orleans. NOLA. The Crescent City. The Big Easy.

How can I possibly begin to describe my favorite city, my birthplace?

New Orleans is a city of love, hope, resilience, and a cuisine as rich as its culture. It is known for its majestic moss-draped trees, which gracefully line the city's Southern architecture, with stunning views of Lake Pontchartrain and the magnificent flow of the mighty Mississippi. The area is famous for Mardi Gras, King Cakes, its rich and layered history, and the mystique of voodoo. As the birthplace of jazz, New Orleans is home to generations of talented singers and musicians who have shared their boundless talents with the world.

New Orleans stands as one of the country's true melting pots. Blacks, Whites, Creoles, Afro-Creoles, Cajuns, Coonasses, Asians, Italians, the French, the Spanish, Latinos, and other Europeans, all interwoven through generations of blending, have poured their hearts into this city and could never imagine calling anyplace else home.

Those in this great city are known for their community spirit and warmth. We love music, we love to party, we love to eat, we love to dance, and we love each other. We greet strangers as we go by, because in New Orleans, when you're here, you're automatically a part of our community. When you visit, we want you to come back. Tourists can experience the city's history through its people, without ever having to open a history book. Our stories have passed down from generation to generation: stories of pain, sorrow, and disappointment, but also stories of love, kindness, and neighbors helping one another. This is who we are.

So, it is no surprise that twenty years after the worst disaster in the annals of the Crescent City, we're still here. While the heart of New Orleans pulses solidly, Hurricane Katrina pierced a hole in its soul in 2005. We were a city of 480,000 strong pre-Katrina; only about 75 percent of the residents have returned since that storm's devastation.[1] Homes in which we grew up and planned to leave for our children and grandchildren have vanished. In a deluge of water and forceful winds, those dwellings were lifted and shifted, downed and drowned, ripped apart board by board, taking with them the precious histories and artifacts of families who settled into this area over two hundred years ago.

Katrina observed an unsuspecting target and hit its bullseye. She entered New Orleans spewing hate, vitriol, and venom. She successfully upended every life and structure that had the unlucky misfortune of being in her path. She dared to test the resilience of this city.

Twenty years later, we are fighting to recover, but at least we are still fighting. No one in this city throws in the towel. We use it to wipe our sweat. Tragedy may bend us, but it will never break us. Not us. New Orleans does not succumb to tragedy. It is not in our makeup, not in our blood.

# Chapter 2
## Life in the Crescent City Pre-Katrina

For as long as I can remember, residents of New Orleans talked about hurricanes as "She's coming and she's a Category 3!" I rarely heard anyone say "it" is coming. There was a silly joke in high school about why hurricanes weren't named after men. The punch line was: "It's because there are no 'himmacanes'!" Men's names were added to the storm rosters in 1979. However, I don't think I've ever referred to a male storm as "He's coming this way."

Before Katrina, New Orleans and the Gulf Coast had weathered many tropical storms and hurricanes. However, the last Category 5 storm was Hurricane Camille, which had winds of 190 mph. She struck the Mississippi Gulf Coast on August 17–18, 1969, causing devastating flooding, even in New Orleans. Camille came thirty-six years before Katrina. Consider that if you were thirty-six or younger in 2005, you had never experienced anything like Camille. You grew up after her, with no social media or constant reminders of what a Category 5 storm could do. So, when these individuals heard Katrina had reached CAT 5 status at one point, how could they realistically picture her wiping out an entire city?

With this history lesson in mind, Friday, August 26, 2005, at 5:00 p.m. should have been a repeat of Fridays in August from years past. Employees would have been readying for a mass exodus from the many downtown high-rise offices, hurrying to beat the long stream of other vehicles starting their commute home.

However, on Friday, August 26, 2005, these residents were NOT downtown working and watching the clock. The high-rises were already vacant, locked down with their windows boarded. No one was thinking about how they would spend the weekend. Everybody already knew.

On August 26, we all woefully discovered the city of New Orleans was now officially in the "dreaded cone" of Hurricane Katrina.

The Weather Channel defines "the cone as representing the most probable track of the center of a tropical depression, storm, or hurricane over the next five days, assuming a storm lasts that long."[2] Now, in real people's terms? Picture a waffle cone with a big scoop of ice cream; this is precisely what the cone looks like, albeit horizontal, not vertical. The pointed bottom represents the current location of the storm. As the waffle cone widens to the opening where the ice cream sits, this growing shape represents the area the path of the storm can take. The storm can either go directly ahead, veer to the north, south, or west, or take an unexpected turn in any of those directions at the very last minute. Meteorologists and other weather officials cannot say with certainty which direction the storm will head because the track is based on so many factors related to nature, such as the temperature of the water in the Gulf, whether there are winds from the north that could affect the hurricane winds, precipitation, wind shear, and so much more.

Weather updates come every few hours, and for residents in all areas of the cone, it's a waiting game. We stay anxious, speculating if the storm is headed our way, and if so, how strong the winds will be when they reach us, and wondering on which side of the storm we will be. If you've ever seen what a hurricane looks like on TV, you'll notice it rotates counterclockwise. The left side is less dangerous (though there's no such thing as a good side) because the right side brings rainstorms to land and causes the dreaded storm surge. Picture surfer waves in Hawaii or California. They're beautiful, right? Not so when they rise ten to twelve feet and then surge over your house, destroying everything you've worked hard for. This is why no area wants to be in the dreaded cone of uncertainty.

State and local officials immediately notify the public if their location falls within the cone of uncertainty, sometimes referred to as the "cone of concern" or the "cone of death." When this happens, bottled water, toilet paper, batteries, and canned goods suddenly disappear from store shelves. Gas stations develop long lines, with irritated consumers wondering exactly how many cans of gasoline the customers ahead of them plan to fill. Sheets of plywood and generators become like gold at home building stores.

On Friday, August 26, 2005, survival mode was in full effect in the Big Easy.

# Chapter 3

## Get Ready, Here She Comes

**National Hurricane Center**

**Weather Report**

**Tuesday, August 23, 2005 ~ 5:00 p.m.**

• Southeastern Bahamas, about 350 miles east of Miami

• Watch: tropical depression forming

**Wednesday, August 24, 2005 ~ 11:00 a.m.**

• 230 miles east of Miami

• Tropical depression upgraded to Tropical Storm Katrina

• Sustained winds 40 miles per hour

**Thursday, August 25, 2005 ~ 5:00 p.m.**

• 15 miles east of Fort Lauderdale

• Tropical Storm Katrina upgraded to Hurricane Katrina, CAT 1

• Sustained winds 75 miles per hour

Within forty-eight hours, Katrina had strengthened from a tropical storm to a hurricane as she made landfall between Fort Lauderdale and North Miami Beach on August 25, 2005. She did not arrive alone. Her entourage consisted of heavy rains, strong winds, sporadic flooding, and power outages.

**National Hurricane Center**
**Weather Report**
**Thursday, August 25, 2005 ~ 5:00 p.m.**
• Official eye of Hurricane Katrina comes ashore between North Miami Beach and Hallandale Beach
• Sustained winds 75 miles per hour

**Friday, August 26, 2005 ~ 1:00 a.m.**
• Center of storm approximately 45 miles from Key Largo
• Katrina downgraded to a tropical storm post-landfall
• Sustained winds 70 miles per hour

What we did not know as we slept through the night (for those of us who slept) was that at around 3:00 a.m., Katrina was crossing the very warm waters of the Gulf of Mexico as she emerged from the Florida peninsula. Those warm waters fed her, and she strengthened immediately.

**National Hurricane Center**

**Weather Report**

**Friday, August 26, 2005 ~ 5:00 a.m.**

• Eye of the storm approximately 70 miles northwest of Key Largo

• Tropical Storm Katrina upgraded to Hurricane Katrina, CAT 1

• Sustained winds 75 miles per hour

**Friday Update ~ 11:30 a.m. (just over six hours later)**

• Sustained winds 100 miles per hour

• Hurricane Katrina upgraded to Category 2

• Storm path projected second landfall along the Gulf Coast of Mississippi and New Orleans

This National Hurricane Center news stunned us. Initial forecasts wrongfully projected that Katrina would hit Florida, then dissipate once she made landfall. Mississippi and Louisiana residents had no reason to expect a direct hit from Katrina. Louisiana Governor Kathleen Blanco and Mississippi Governor Haley Barbour declared a state of emergency in each of their respective states in response.

On Friday, August 26, 2005, at approximately 11:00 p.m., the National Hurricane Center predicted Katrina would become a major hurricane by the time she reached the central Gulf of Mexico. By now, the eye of the storm was about 460 miles southeast of the mouth of the Mississippi River.

Many New Orleans city officials and first responders were taken aback. Once Katrina's track was confirmed on August 26,

2005, a state of emergency was immediately declared for the city of New Orleans. The unexpected arrival of this very unwelcome guest created contagious anxiety. Those residents in the fortunate position to evacuate immediately were encouraged (although not mandated at this time) to do so by New Orleans' Mayor Clarence "Ray" Nagin, as well as the many newscasters and meteorologists covering the story of this impending disaster on a 24/7 basis. However, by the time the storm's direction was established, it was too late to put together a massive evacuation process that would be effective.

**National Hurricane Center**
**Weather Report**
**Saturday, August 27, 2005 ~ 5:00 am**
Hurricane Katrina upgraded to Category 3
sustained winds 115 miles per hour.

With less than three days before Katrina was expected to make landfall on the Louisiana coast, Interstate 10 was already bursting at the seams with a mass exodus of vehicles traveling at an average speed of 0 mph. Residents were unable to travel along the coastal areas because that would have brought them directly into the path of Katrina. Others who could not leave so easily, such as residents without reliable transportation, older people, or those lacking the financial means for travel, were now relying on the mayor to provide some shelter of last resort for them to hunker down until Katrina made her departure.

As the residents of the entire Gulf Region were glued to their televisions, watching the news and weather reports, prayers were plentiful. Residents, relatives, friends, and strangers alike were wishing, waiting, and hoping for a miracle. We prayed that somehow the approaching storm would perform a "stage left" and veer off into the Gulf without affecting any communities.

It was not unusual for me to find myself alone during hurricane season. As the residents of New Orleans planned their exit strategy, my husband was already working to assist in prepping the city. As a retired Hurricane Hunter in the Air Force Reserve, he also worked with Entergy, the area's major utility company. He, along with other supervisors and city officials, was coordinating a staging area in the eastern part of the city, routing trucks out of the town before the storm so they could return post-storm to repair power sources lost due to fallen trees and other storm hazards. He usually left the house at 6:30 a.m. for work, but with storm duty, he had to leave at 5:00 a.m. every morning that week.

When my husband called me at home that Friday around 1:00 p.m., he was upset to learn that I had not yet evacuated. He called me on the home phone. I probably shouldn't have answered. Busted!

"What are you still doing at home?"

I cautiously responded, "Getting some things together: your parents' picture, our wedding pictures, and some supplies."

He was not happy. I could hear the deep sigh on the other end of the line. He knew that he had made it clear to me that I should have long since been on the road, but this was not an "I told you so" moment. He took a breath, and he spoke in as calm a voice as he could.

"Well, you need to get going. I thought you had already left."

I did not want to lie to him, so I responded, "As soon as I get some things together, I'm going to head out. I'm not taking the interstate. I'm taking the back way. I will let you know when I'm on the road, or at least when I get to Belle Rose."

My goal was to reassure him that I would be leaving soon. The truth is that I was nowhere near ready to go, but at that point, it did not make sense for me to cause him any additional worry. I justified in my mind that "soon" meant I would be leaving within an hour or two, but I knew that his definition of "soon" was more like ten or fifteen minutes, at the maximum.

Because of the projected magnitude of Katrina, I decided to board up our windows. On early Friday morning, I joined my fellow New Orleanians in a long but progressively shifting line at Home Depot. I purchased fiberboards, 2x4s, a hammer, nails, and electric saw blades. I had never used an electric saw in my life, but I had watched enough episodes of *This Old House* to give it a try. I couldn't tell my husband about my plans because just days before, I nearly cut off the tip of my thumb while using a cheese grater!

At Home Depot, I felt like a ship out of water among the many experienced carpenters and confident woodworkers in line, as I prayed that I could figure out what I needed to do to preserve our home. I received unexpected assistance from a kind gentleman who was also getting his supplies. Although no one was conversing in line, this gentleman out of nowhere began chatting with me.

"You're getting supplies?"

I responded nervously in the affirmative.

It felt as though he could see straight through me, sensing the weight of the task I had brought upon myself.

His name was Ray, and he donned a pair of very worn Levi's with an Oakland Raiders tee shirt and a Saints baseball cap. He told me how the Raiders became his favorite AFC team and the Saints his favorite NFC team. We chatted the entire time in line. His southern twang was prevalent. "Now, ma'am, it's real important, I mean real important, that you measure twice, not once, before you cut. Because if not, you're gonna be wasting some good materials, and you're not gonna have any good materials to waste!" Once home, I proceeded to measure, measure, cut, place boards, hammer, measure, measure, cut, place boards, hammer. And finally, measure once, measure twice, cut, place boards, hammer, and my first-floor windows were secure. I remember being extremely calm performing these tasks, as if I had done them many times before.

Even though Ray's advice was simple, his calm demeanor and quiet care comforted me. He recognized my unease and fear, and in that moment, he became a perfect example of the little miracles we often overlook and forget to celebrate.

Reflecting on Ray's assistance, I was comfortable that I had done everything according to his instructions. But now it was time to evacuate. I had a very sick feeling in my stomach as I was preparing to leave the house. "Lord, I hope I can come back to this house in its same condition," I prayed. Since returning to New Orleans from California in 1997, I had weathered many hurricanes and tropical storms. Even with the mandatory evacuations, none ever carried the same heavy sense of dread and foreboding as Katrina.

**National Hurricane Center**

**Weather Report**

**Sunday, August 28, 2005 ~ 2:00 a.m.**

• Hurricane Katrina upgraded to Category 4

• Sustained winds 145 miles per hour

• 310 miles south of the Mississippi River

**Sunday, August 28, 2005 ~ 11:00 a.m.**

• Hurricane Katrina upgraded to Category 5

• Sustained winds 175 miles per hour

• Eye of the storm 225 miles from the mouth of the Mississippi River

**Sunday, August 28, 2005 ~ 5:00 p.m.**

• Katrina described as a "potentially catastrophic" hurricane by the National Hurricane Center

Sunday, August 29, 2005, at approximately 9:30 a.m., Mayor Nagin issued a mandatory evacuation order for New Orleans. This was when we undoubtedly knew the storm's track was coming straight for us. It was the reality check many residents needed to reconsider their decision to shelter in place or not. Looking at the massive girth of this storm was more than the average person could fathom.

We were SO screwed!

# Chapter 4
## The Shelters of Last Resort and Lost Hope

The evacuation was a fluctuating combination of adequate panicking and inadequate planning.

There was, at least on paper, an evacuation plan in place. Residents were instructed to drive north or west, using the "contraflow" system, which was designed to keep traffic moving steadily out of the city. Contraflow temporarily reverses the inbound lanes, converting them into outbound lanes, allowing more evacuees to escape at once. The system was first implemented in 1998 during Hurricane Georges, but it required at least seventy-two hours of advance notice to function correctly.

During Katrina, however, the evacuation order came too late. With only a short window before landfall, traffic quickly clogged the highways, gas stations ran out of fuel, and thousands of residents without vehicles or means of transportation were left stranded. These breakdowns highlighted the limits of contraflow in a large-scale disaster and the lack of resources to support those unable to go on their own. The system has not been used since Katrina.

The system's inefficiency revealed more than just logistical problems. Divisions among residents became painfully apparent. Those with the resources to leave did so, while those without the means to escape faced an unimaginable fate.

Interstates 10 and 12 were the only multi-lane, viable routes to Baton Rouge. Residents from Orleans, Jefferson, St. Bernard, and other surrounding parishes on the south shore of Lake Pontchartrain accessed Interstate 10. Residents from St. Tammany and Tangipahoa parishes on the north shore of Lake Pontchartrain used Interstate 12 to travel to Baton Rouge. Due to the inefficient loading of the contraflow from New Orleans, the lack of accurate traffic information, and the high number of evacuees, a major bottleneck formed on Interstate 10, discouraging many last-minute evacuees from attempting to leave. Evacuees were encouraged by state officials to use alternative routes, such as I-10 West to I-55 North to Mississippi, Highway 90 West to Baton Rouge, and other local highways.

One of the city council members had worked with the local Regional Transit Authority (RTA) to ensure buses would be available at key pickup locations to transport citizens to safety. The evacuees were instructed to bring supplies, specifically sleeping bags, drinking water, and at least three days of food. The buses were to drive about two hours north of New Orleans, around where Interstate 10 connects with Interstate 12 near Baton Rouge, where shelters had been set up and were prepared to accommodate the evacuees. However, these plans were changed due to the massive exodus from the city. The Office of Emergency Preparedness decided on August 28, the day before landfall, that it would be better to take residents to a shelter in New Orleans rather than attempt the drive to Baton Rouge. The evacuees would spend the night in the city to weather the storm; afterwards, on August 30, the buses would take them to the Baton Rouge shelters.

The chosen shelter in New Orleans was the Louisiana Superdome, then known as the Caesars Superdome. Once word of mouth spread throughout the city, residents who had not yet left or lacked the means to do so began showing up at the Superdome. It was described as a "refuge of last resort." Mayor Nagin held several press conferences in the days leading up to Katrina's landfall, advising that there would be no refuges of last resort. He encouraged everyone to leave. Yet, on Sunday, August 28, at 9:30 a.m. CDT, he announced:

"Ladies and gentlemen, we are facing a storm that most of us have feared."[3]

He advised during this press conference that the Superdome would be opening to individuals with special needs, i.e., those requiring dialysis, individuals in wheelchairs, and others for whom travel was not feasible. As of noon on that day, the Superdome would be available to anyone who needed to find a refuge of last resort. But he cautioned: "Let me emphasize: the first choice of every citizen is to figure out a way to leave the city. I'm asking all the churches; we sent out faxes to all the churches that we could this morning, asking them to buddy up, to find members of their congregations to check on senior citizens, or citizens who may not have the means, and are relying upon public transportation."[4]

Mayor Nagin announced that the city, working with the RTA, would provide free bus service throughout the day to transport residents needing a last resort refuge to the Superdome. Ten pickup sites were designated, many of which were located in low-lying neighborhoods where large numbers of residents of color resided. The choice of these sites underscored the city's longstanding inequities, that those most vulnerable to flooding were also those with the fewest resources to evacuate on their own.

Additionally, he gave this predictive warning to anyone who planned to take shelter in the Superdome: "Keep in mind, a hurricane, a Category 5, with high winds, most likely will knock out all the electricity in the city; therefore, the Superdome is not going to be a very comfortable place at some point in time. So, we are encouraging everyone to leave!"

Once that last-minute decision was announced on local TV stations, thousands of residents entered the Superdome in anticipation of riding out the storm overnight with plans to return to their homes within the next two days. The Superdome had a capacity of approximately 60,000 people in 2005, according to multiple sources, and the estimated number of individuals seeking shelter there was between 20,000 and 30,000[5]. Being overcrowded was not the issue. The lines were extremely long for individuals to enter the facility, stretching as far as a quarter mile at one point. Security checked everyone's bags, so it took a long time for the residents to enter. Still, the citizens were relieved to be able to ride out the storm at the Superdome. What could be safer than the city's largest and most structurally sound structure? After all, this was the home of the New Orleans Saints!

Families found pockets of seats where they huddled together, and if they happened to see friends, they invited them into their group. Initially, the electricity was on, and the plumbing worked efficiently. At half capacity, the residents felt comfortable and believed that once the storm passed, they would be able to head home. On Sunday, once everyone had entered the facility, there was a sense of relief. It was sorely misplaced.

Katrina crashed into downtown New Orleans the morning of August 29, and, within minutes of her arrival, she made her presence known angrily and viciously. The winds howled, pushing sheets of rain visible through the Superdome's windows, as the humid air seeped in through the many entrances. As Mayor Nagin predicted, the turbulent winds downed electrical lines that morning, and the Superdome lost power. As the hours loomed, the conditions in the arena deteriorated.

With no power, there was no air conditioning. It was a sweltering August day, reportedly in the 90s, in a building with no circulating air. The stench of sweat permeated throughout the structure. The roof began to leak almost immediately. First came droplets, then drizzles, which were not alarming. Then, as the evacuees heard a piercing yet shredding rumble, the startled occupants looked up and watched in terror as a large part of the Superdome's majestic roof was mangled off by the hammering winds, immediately flooding parts of the dome with torrents of showers. The frightened citizens were forced to hastily grab their belongings and scramble to another area of the facility for safety.

Although food was provided on August 28, it became scarce very quickly. The water in the building had stopped running, leaving residents of the dome miserably hot, hungry, and thirsty. The restroom conditions had also worsened. Toilets soon began to overflow and couldn't be flushed, and there was no replacement tissue or other restroom supplies available. The back-up generators were able to run the lights, but not much more. Without its regular electricity, the air conditioning system and the refrigeration system that kept massive amounts of food cold were no longer working. Food was spoiling. It was pitch black in some areas of the Superdome, where the lighting had sustained the most damage. Residents of the structure used their personal flashlights and cell phones as needed for light.

Those with radios learned about some of the twenty-eight levee breaches on the morning of Katrina's landfall. They discovered the buses scheduled to take them to Baton Rouge were all underwater. The news traveled quickly, and all found themselves captured in this 680,000-square-foot prison cell, with its severely impacted roof, the stench of rotting food, despicable smells from the restrooms and other areas where individuals took relief, with no hope of being paroled anytime soon. Many described their ordeal as the equivalent of living in a third-world country. The conditions were progressively deplorable.

In addition to the Superdome, the Ernest M. Morial Convention Center, located at the riverbank just over a mile from the home of the Saints, was also not scheduled to be opened as a shelter of last resort. The breach of the levees changed all that.

I cannot say with certainty how many people the convention center can accommodate. However, with a staggering 1.1 million square feet and nearly a mile long, this magnificent facility near the Mississippi River has housed many conferences simultaneously, including the Mardi Gras Orpheus Ball, where massive floats can drive into the actual ball, accompanied by high school, college, and military bands, to entertain the excited and exquisitely dressed guests.[6] On the day of the storm, though, there were about forty essential convention center workers, who either volunteered to remain at the center or were mandated to be there, including the center's president, Jimmie Fore, along with about three hundred other employees and their families.

Initially, approximately 1,000 people gathered outside the convention center at a selected pickup point. They were waiting for buses to take them out of downtown New Orleans to designated shelters. Sadly, due to a series of misfires, the buses never arrived, and these individuals never received notification about the issue. As they waited for transportation that would never come, they began to panic and asked for entry into the convention center. Mr. Fore made a plea to these people, telling them that the center was not a viable shelter; that there was no food, water, electricity, medical care, or any other provisions that shelters typically provide. His pleas were brushed aside, however.

The security guards locked the doors and turned their backs to the desperate evacuees. They, in turn, yanked on the doors in response and, with force, managed to break the lock on one of them, gaining entry. They soon discovered that Mr. Fore's statement was forthright. There were no provisions in place. There was no food available. There were no comfortable chairs spread out for people to sit on. There was no bottled water available for distribution. People were in this vast, hollow shell of a building that served two purposes on the night of Katrina—to keep people from being soaked by the torrential rains, and to keep them from drowning in their own homes.

Once a gleaming showcase of architectural glamour, the convention center became, under Katrina's wrath, a hollow matchbox of steel, brick, and glass, with thousands of souls jammed inside, struck against despair like sparks waiting to ignite.

Sadly, as the night continued, the convention center inhabitants found themselves in the same situation as the occupants of the Superdome. While the buildings withstood the storm, there was no electricity, no water, no food, no facilities, plus no one in authority to maintain any civility or enforce any laws, rules, or regulations.

Those stuck in their homes were not free from danger, either. They went to bed hunkered down, praying for only heavy winds and mild flooding. On August 29, they woke to find deep water in their homes, especially those in the lowest-lying areas of New Orleans, the result of the unimaginable levee breaches. It was apparent the water would continue to rise, and their only option was to leave their homes for safety. Folks grabbed what they could and found themselves wading, walking, or swimming to downtown New Orleans, heading to the Superdome, unaware of the drama unfolding there. Upon arrival, however, they were turned away, left without transportation to serve them, and with nowhere else to go. The only advice the officials at the Superdome could offer was that perhaps these evacuees could find shelter at the Ernest M. Morial Convention Center.

So, in addition to the miles already walked, evacuees were now told they had to walk an extra mile to the Convention Center. What would typically take fifteen to twenty minutes stretched into what felt like forever, as families struggled through the flooded sections of Poydras Avenue, the main boulevard linking the Superdome and the Convention Center. Many were unprepared for the flooding near their beds; some wore slippers, house shoes, or, if fortunate, tennis shoes. They navigated broken glass, mud, debris, and stagnant water, believing they were heading toward safety, only to discover that conditions at the Convention Center were just as unbearable as if they had stayed in their powerless, sweltering homes without food or water. Most carried whatever they could snatch from home, stuffed into garbage bags, cradling babies and toddlers in their arms, while helping their elderly relatives navigate along in a trudging march to Hell under the brutal 90–95° heat.

The residents of the Superdome and the Convention Center were not the only ones in danger. During Katrina, fifty-two nursing homes operated in New Orleans. The Louisiana Nursing Home Association recommended that all facilities evacuate two days before the storm. However, there was no coordinated effort to move residents to safety through a unified plan. Each nursing home was clearly informed that it was responsible for its own evacuation. Out of the fifty-two homes, only seventeen managed to evacuate their residents. Families were devastated to discover their loved ones had not been evacuated, and some were overwhelmed by the fact that their loved ones had not survived. Lives were lost among residents and staff, and the blame game, along with extensive lawsuits, continued for many months after Katrina.

Healthcare workers who chose to stay with their patients did their best to remain with them for as long as possible. Some were forced to go home reluctantly, as they had to ensure the safety of their own families, but many opted to stay with the residents of the senior homes, with whom they had become deeply attached. I have watched interviews with some of these selfless people, and they are still burdened with this experience.

As those of us who managed to evacuate in time to Belle Rose heard these horrible stories, watching live reports on the local news channels, we thanked God we were able to leave in time. My family would soon learn, though, that we had family members in both locations. Cousin Geraldine Levy and her family sought shelter in the Superdome, and Cousin Monica's in-laws, Arthur and Bernadine Moran, were transported to the Convention Center.

And with this, little miracles begin....

# Chapter 5

## The Morans' Unconventional Rescue

Have you ever met a couple where you could feel an unbreakable bond? That you just knew they had faced their trials and tribulations together and emerged with even more love? That you knew they not only loved each other but were still deeply in love? If so, then you would know I am describing Arthur and Bernadine Moran, the in-laws of my cousin Monica.

I had met the Morans on several occasions while attending family gatherings hosted by Monica. Monica had a spacious, designer home in the quaint, little city of Belle Rose. Over the years, she often opened her doors to family members seeking shelter from approaching hurricanes. Monica was a widow with two daughters, and her mother also lived with her. Even with four people in the house, Monica could still accommodate another six to eight individuals. During hurricane season, there was no shortage of evacuees seeking shelter in her home on Ideal Street. However, in the case of Hurricane Katrina, the Morans did not leave New Orleans in time to find safety with their daughter-in-law.

Mr. and Mrs. Moran were a dignified couple in their early sixties. They were high school sweethearts; both attended Booker T. Washington High School in New Orleans. Arthur graduated from Southern University of New Orleans and was a Navy veteran. After discharge, he started a successful career with the United

States Postal Service, where he worked until retirement. Bernadine was a graduate of the Charity School of Surgical Technology, and she spent her career working in Labor and Delivery at Methodist Hospital in New Orleans East, retiring from that position. They regularly attended church. They were simply one of those couples that when you saw one, you saw the other. I don't know exactly how long they had been married, but I would say at least forty years at the time of the storm, and yet, they still presented themselves very much like newlyweds.

I always thought Bernadine had the most beautiful chestnut skin. Her nails were always meticulously manicured and polished, and there was never a hair out of place. Arthur would show up in a nice polo shirt and slacks. I don't believe I ever saw either of them in denim. They were always dressed to impress. They didn't do this to show off; it was simply who they were. They were very personable, likable, and affectionate. They always gave big hugs to everyone.

That's why it wasn't a surprise to us when Bernadine's mental state was so fragile when she called Monica's house on September 1, three days after Katrina, begging for someone to come to Algiers, a city just west of New Orleans across the Mississippi River, to pick them up from an amphibious battleship where they had sought refuge. This is where I stepped in.

Because Monica had to work and couldn't take time off to rescue her in-laws, I volunteered to pick up the Morans, paying it forward to Monica for letting my three cats and I stay at her home during the storm. Monica's sister-in-law, Angela Johnson, wife of Monica's brother, Cordell, offered to go with me. The family thought it would be safer for two people to make that long trip, considering the stories we heard about lootings and carjackings. We all imagined the desperation of people trying to escape chaos, to find food and water, and to survive.

Monica spoke directly to her in-laws, and they explained they were currently on a naval ship called the USS Iwo Jima. The Morans had managed to catch a ride to the boat from the Morial Convention Center. We did not have any additional details, but we would soon learn that the Morans' journey was just as miraculous as their rescue.

The ship was stationed in Algiers, Louisiana, about 70 miles from Belle Rose, and the drive took roughly 90 minutes. NBC News later reported that gasoline prices had jumped by as much as $0.40 per gallon the day after the storm, a result of massive disruptions in oil production across the Gulf of Mexico. At the time, we didn't realize this was only the beginning of a sharp, ongoing rise in fuel prices after Katrina. In 2005, hybrids and electric vehicles were rare, so Angela offered to drive us in her spacious Dodge Durango. I took on the responsibility of planning the trip so we wouldn't get lost. With satellites down, GPS was useless, but I had always taken pride in reading maps in the old-fashioned way. Confidently, I directed Angela toward Highway LA 3127, a 42.1-mile state highway stretching from Donaldsonville to

Boutte, just west of New Orleans. From there, we would take Highway 90 for about 40 miles to reach the port.

We were not alone on our journey from LA 3127 to Hwy 90 by any means. Dozens of commercial, military, and passenger vehicles shared the road with us. This gave us a sense of relief, confirming that the roads were open, at least to get close to New Orleans. However, as we neared the entrance to Highway 90, traffic came to a complete standstill.

Because we were behind military vehicles, we couldn't see exactly what was causing the traffic delay, so I got out of the passenger seat to take a look. All military and commercial vehicles were directed to move to the left lane, while the state troopers signaled all non-commercial and passenger vehicles to the right. Before I got back into the car, I estimated that there were at least fifteen or twenty non-commercial vehicles in the lane we would eventually end up in. The troopers allowed all commercial and military vehicles to continue to their destinations but stopped all passenger vehicles.

This was the first moment of anxiety for us both as we watched every single passenger vehicle turn around.

Stunned by what I was witnessing, all I could say was, "Uh oh!" I stood out of the vehicle and joined Angela on the left side of the Durango. I shared my observations and returned to the car.

We sat quietly for a minute, either waiting to see at least one car get through. None did. I sighed and, with a look of dismay, said, "Angie, they're turning everyone around. Lord have mercy, we might not even get through."

My usual exclamation of frustration slipped out: "Crap!"

Angie let out a big sigh and shook her head no. "Girl, I hope we didn't make this long-ass ride for nothing."

I couldn't find any encouragement because I wasn't feeling it. So, I just said matter-of-factly, "Well, I guess we will know soon enough."

I was holding my piece of paper with the ship's name on it. I had practiced all morning on how to say it right. I wanted to make sure I pronounced "Iwo Jima" with the "I" as in "I," not as in "E." When we approached the state trooper, Angela pressed the power button to roll down the driver's side window. The officer was waiting to talk to us. He wasn't friend or foe; he was just expressionless. Before he could say anything, I took the lead. Why not? Let's get this party started, one way or another.

Angie leaned back, and from the passenger side, I leaned forward, closer to Angie so he could see and hear me. He was holding a flashlight, which was odd because it was broad daylight.

"Hello, Officer, we are heading to Algiers…"

He nodded and directed his flashlight toward the commercial vehicles.

"Proceed!"

*Huh?*

Observing our utterly puzzled looks, he repeated his instructions, with a bit more authority, "Proceed!"

Shocked, I said, "Thank you!"

Angie sat there for a few moments, stunned.

With raised eyebrows, I prompted, "Angie, go!"

I pushed her arm, not wanting to give the officer even a moment to change his mind. She quickly rolled up her window, shifted the transmission into drive, and "sped off." As we drove away, we exchanged very puzzled looks, then burst into big smiles!

With hysterical laughter, I said, "Oh my God, Angie, we got through! We frigging got through! And we didn't even finish telling him where we were going and what we were doing!"

My chuckling was contagious because she joined me, saying, "I know! I'm shocked! This is too funny!"

As we joined the cavalry of military vehicles that had gained access to Highway 90, I exclaimed, "Man, I don't even believe this! Can you believe we got through?"

She chimed in, "Girl, we must have honest faces or something!"

We both chuckled as I agreed, "I guess!"

What we didn't realize at the time was that we had picked up another passenger – *Bewilderment!*

Angie and I thought the conversation was over, but it was far from truly ending. Angie's curious mind was replaying the incident in her head. Two minutes later: "Vanessa, did he even ask you the name of the ship?"

"No. And I practiced saying the name of that damn ship all morning!" I chuckled, surprised by that fact. "I mean, he didn't ask us anything! Nothing! And it wasn't like someone had called him to tell him who we were or where we were going. It doesn't make sense. I know doggone well that some of these folks ahead of us, who got turned around, were probably trying to do the same thing we're doing, trying to pick up people who needed to get to safety. Right? We can't be the only ones on a mission to rescue folks and get them out of there."

Angie shrugged her shoulders. "Girl, all I can say is that we got through. For whatever reason, we managed to get through. The Lord must have been with us, because I just knew we were going to be turning around!"

"God is definitely our co-pilot today!" I exclaimed.

Angie agreed and added, "Every day."

I don't know how we managed to get past the barricade, but we did. I can't say that I don't understand why we got through. In retrospect, we were able to get through because the path was cleared for us long before we arrived. We went through when every other non-commercial vehicle ahead of us did not. The trooper didn't ask for identification. He didn't wait for me to provide details. We had no valid military or first responder credentials whatsoever. The only word he said was "Proceed." Only by God's grace were we able to continue our purpose-driven mission to rescue the Morans.

As we embarked on the balance of this journey, we initially attributed our success in bypassing the checkpoint to luck or a fluke. But through the eyes and expressions of others, as we have shared our story, we know that this was so much more. A higher power navigated our trip from the moment that we began our journey. And this miraculous journey was just the beginning.

Having received this unexpected little miracle from above, we headed toward Algiers to rescue Mr. and Mrs. Moran. As we entered Marrero on Highway 90, we saw at least forty or fifty government vehicles rushing past us at breakneck speed. Some were clearly members of the National Guard, some were from Wildlife and Fisheries, and others belonged to various law enforcement agencies. They were in a huge hurry to get somewhere.

Angie is a more aggressive driver than I am, but even she felt a little intimidated by how fast those military and commercial vehicles were moving. It was "whoosh, whoosh, whoosh" as they zoomed past us in a blur. Many military vehicles were loaded with troops in their fatigues. Seeing those National Guardsmen on the backs of those trucks in uniform with their huge rifles was also very alarming. This was a world neither Angie nor I knew anything about.

"Girl, this is scary," I said nervously. "I've never seen so many official vehicles at once in my life. They're driving like maniacs, so stay in the right lane, set the cruise control, and let them zoom past us."

At one point, everyone on the road was stopped again. For a moment, Angie and I looked at each other, wondering if there was yet another barricade we would have to try to get through. However, the traffic was only halted to allow certain other vehicles onto the highway, and within minutes, the flow of traffic resumed. As we reached this temporary stop, a truckload of National Guardsmen pulled up beside us on the left. Angie noticed the height of one of the rifles compared to the guard standing next to it. In a mix of fear and awe, Angie asked, "Do you see the size of those rifles on the back of that truck?"

With eyebrows raised, I responded, "Yup. Don't want them to aim those bad boys at us, so let's just keep a low profile. I'm not even about to look in their direction!"

As we traveled through the cities of Marrero, Harvey, and Gretna, en route to Algiers, we finally caught our first glimpse of Katrina's fury. We could see there had been some significant wind damage, but it still looked like the people in those areas could recover with a moderate amount of cleanup once electricity was restored. However, it was the absence of people and the silence that shocked us. The deafening silence. That spoke louder than any rock concert I had ever attended.

As we approached the city of Algiers, just across the Mississippi River from New Orleans, the harsh reality of Hurricane Katrina hit us both. We looked around, beginning to grasp the extent of the damage caused by a Category 3 hurricane compared to what we hear in news reports. Algiers had suffered a relatively severe blow. The large canopies of service stations were completely ripped off, and a Shell Oil canopy had even landed half a block away from the gas station, in the middle of the road on the opposite side of the street.

  Finally, we reached the entrance to the Algiers Naval Base and were greeted by a naval ensign. He was well-trained in the art of service, his expressionless face asking for identification from both of us. We told him we were there to pick up family members from the USS Iwo Jima. After returning our IDs, the ensign signaled for us to enter the base without incident.

  As we parked, I pointed out the levee to Angela, where the USS Iwo Jima floated on the other side. The levee was about forty yards away, so we had a good walk ahead of us. I grew up just half a block from a levee, and the kids in our neighborhood played on that levee all the time. When I was twelve, my friend and I decided to go for a bike ride down the levee together, and I was the dingdong who decided to ride on the handlebars. Well, that didn't last long. About halfway down, she lost control, and I went flying off the bike and onto some rocks. I busted my lip, knee, and elbow. So, I know exactly what levees are built for, and what they're NOT built for, which is to send me home covered in blood, tears, and a busted knee. It was at least comforting to see that the Algiers levee was still intact.

  As we walked closer and looked toward the far right, maybe about thirty yards away, we saw the Morans standing on the levee, anxiously waiting for whoever was coming to take them away from this nightmare. Despite their dangerous journey, they remained as loving as ever. Arthur's arm was around Bernadine's shoulder, and her arm was around his waist, simply holding each other supportively. Waiting. Waiting. Finally, their wait was over.

They saw us as we reached the top of the levee. For a moment, they stayed still. They weren't sure if we were the ones picking them up since it had been a while since they had seen either of us at a family event. We waved to them with forced smiles because we had gone through our own trauma, and we knew theirs had been much worse. Once we were recognized, the couple walked quickly toward us. We all moved closer: first Bernadine to Angie and Arthur to me, then Arthur to Angie and Bernadine to me, exchanging hugs. She almost collapsed in my arms, but Arthur was there to steady her. Both of them looked very tired and weak. Bernadine held tightly to my arm as I helped her down the embankment and to the car. Neither of them talked much during the ride to Belle Rose. I glanced back now and then, seeing him holding her on his chest while she slept. They had been rescued, and their relief was palpable.

While Angie and I were picking up the Morans, Cousin Monica visited the local Walmart and bought some loose-fitting shirts, pants, and undergarments for her in-laws to change into after they arrived and showered. Unaware of this, I asked Bernadine if she needed any clothes since we were about the same size. I also asked if she wanted me to wash the clothes that she and Arthur were wearing.

She exclaimed passionately, "No, burn them. I never want to see them again!" It wasn't the clothing that Bernadine was rejecting. It was the nightmare that was stitched into every thread.

Later, when we all sat in Monica's living room discussing their experience, the Morans shared their incredible story.

The Morans lived in the eastern part of New Orleans, affectionately called "New Orleans East." Some areas of New Orleans East are prone to flooding, so these residents typically evacuate. The Morans usually checked into a hotel, or sometimes Bernadine volunteered to stay at her workplace, Baptist Hospital, where she worked as a surgical technician at that time. The hospital is located on Napoleon Avenue in the uptown area of the city; an area that rarely, if ever, floods. During Katrina, the Morans decided to stay at Baptist Hospital, believing that, like everyone else, they would be able to return home within a day or two.

However, Katrina was not selective about where she caused damage. During the first night, the hospital suffered extensive wind damage from gusts so strong they shattered many windows throughout the building, including the walkway between the main hospital and the convalescent center. Shortly after the windows broke, the facility lost power. The generators started providing enough light for staff to navigate the building and keep essential equipment running; however, because they had limited capacity and focused only on the patients and hospital equipment, there was not enough electricity to run the air conditioning and refrigerators.

Despite this, the staff was concerned but not panicked, believing it would be a 24 to 48-hour ordeal. Although the building shook more than ever during the storm and there were serious worries it might not withstand the gusts, the winds eased and the rain slowed. The staff, patients, parents of newborns, and family members sheltering with them let out a sigh of relief, trusting they had weathered the storm.

"Or so they believed," relayed Bernadine. No one could imagine that within a few hours, the entire area would be flooded, turning their initial relief and joy into unexpected horror and panic.

Arthur and Bernadine made it safe through the night of August 29. The next morning, they discussed when they might go home, feeling relieved and hopeful. Communication was nearly impossible then because Katrina's winds had knocked down many cell towers, and most parts of the city had no power. So, they decided to wait another day before heading home, hoping for restored cell phone service or some form of media news if the hospital technicians could manage to set up communication with the outside.

That Tuesday at midday, Arthur and Bernadine took a walk up Claiborne Avenue, the wide thoroughfare that stretches across the city for miles. They headed north toward downtown, enjoying the fresh air and talking about their return home. The hospital was only two blocks behind them, close enough to feel safe. What they didn't realize was that floodwater was approaching the very place they stood. As they strolled casually, they noticed the mood around them change. Cars and trucks rushed past toward the hospital, while people on foot and bikes hurried in the same direction, calling out warnings as they went.

"The city is flooding! The city is flooding! You've gotta find high ground! You've gotta find high ground!"

Arthur and Bernadine were stunned. It made no sense. Where was this water coming from? Then, as they looked toward the downtown area, they saw thin, unexpected streams beginning to creep their way toward them.

Without hesitation, they headed back toward the hospital, quickening their pace. Better to escape any danger, even if the warnings seemed exaggerated. By the time they returned, they learned that several levees had broken. The hospital was once again in chaos. Staff worried about their safety and the patients in both the main hospital and the convalescent center. A bigger concern was the generators and food supplies, all stored on the lower level. Teams hurried to bring food upstairs, but the heavy generators couldn't be moved. The only hope was that the water would stay below four feet; if it rose higher, the hospital's power, and survival, would be at risk.

Non-essential personnel and their families were given the option to leave the facility. The hospital learned that high-water military vehicles were arriving at various hospitals and other health centers to rescue patients, staff, and family members and bring them to higher ground. The Morans managed to secure a way out of the hospital and were taken to the Morial Convention Center, which had become an involuntary shelter of last resort.

This is where their true nightmare starts.

From the moment the Morans were dropped off, a clear case of infectious chaos was already taking root. The convention center had never been meant as a shelter of last resort, so no systems existed, no housing, no food, no sanitation. The oppressive heat only worsened everything. The evacuees inside were left irritable, restless, frightened, hungry, and desperate.

With no system in place, survival became a matter of instinct. People searched desperately for water, scraps of food, or a place to rest. The air was thick with heat, fear, and the pungent smell of too many people packed into one space, with no relief in sight. Arthur and Bernadine tried to steady each other, but it was impossible to ignore the growing desperation that seemed to echo off the walls.

The Morans, like many others, kept to themselves and stayed under the radar. The conditions were terrible. Arthur would escort Bernadine to the ladies' room, which was filthy, and he would check the bathroom before she went in. They had to walk over dirty floors and deal with other situations I prefer not to mention, but you get the general idea.

Due to the chaos and mayhem inside the convention center, Arthur and Bernadine spent most of their time outside, even though the heat was nearly unbearable. Bernadine said she needed to breathe and that it was impossible to do that inside "that place."

After sharing their Katrina story to this point, Bernadine began telling the family members the most amazing story. I will relate it to you in her voice.

We stepped outside on our second full day there, thinking about how we could escape this hell. There had to be a way out. We knew we weren't the only ones trying to leave, and we saw that whenever a vehicle approached the convention center, crowds of people from the facility rushed to the car, begging and pleading for help. We understood that even if help arrived, we probably wouldn't be among the first rescued. There were too many others in greater need than we were.

As we walked through the corridor yesterday, a young woman approached us. I had seen her staring at us earlier, but I thought maybe she thought she knew us; that perhaps she also came from the hospital, but I did not recall having seen her in the facility or on the military rescue vehicle. Usually, I would smile and say hello, but I couldn't do it. Nothing against her, but smiling was simply out of the question at that moment.

The young woman was Caucasian and seemed to be alone. She was very attractive, likely in her mid-twenties, and looked visibly scared, trembling. It was clear she didn't blend in. She looked at me with a nervous smile, and I responded in kind.

She approached us carefully, and we began with a casual conversation.

I asked her if she was okay, already knowing the answer just by looking at her.

She said she was feeling overwhelmed by everything.

I agreed and told her that we'd never experienced anything like this before.

From there, we began talking and we introduced ourselves. Her name was Nicole.

She startled me by grabbing my hand and, with tear-filled eyes, begged, "Would you mind if I remain near the two of you until the rescuers arrive? I'm afraid. I'm not prejudiced, I promise. It's just that I'm not used to being by myself in big crowds like this, and I'm terrified. I do not know anyone here, and I am hearing stories that are making me very, very nervous."

Of course, I told her she was welcome to stay with us. I assured her she would come through this safely when we did. Little did we know that she would be the one to lead us to safety.

Monica's living room was silent as Bernadine shared her story. There were at least six or eight of us in the room listening, and none of us moved, asked questions, or interrupted Bernadine. Her voice was steady, but the weight of her words filled the room. We leaned in without realizing it, caught by the rawness of her experience. She went on to say:

Nobody had working cell phones at the convention center, so I am not sure how Nicole was able to reach her husband. But the next morning, she was awake when I opened my eyes, and she told Arthur and me the most incredible news. Her husband was an ensign on the Navy ship, USS Iwo Jima, which was docked right over in Algiers. Somehow, she managed to contact him and inform him of her location. She never went into detail about how that call happened, and with everything going on, Arthur and I didn't think to ask. Nicole's husband had given her a time and place for pickup and told her to be there; he and a shipmate would come to get her. She told him all about us, and he agreed to bring a vehicle that could accommodate all five of us.

Somehow, he managed to get his hands on a working USPS mail truck and drove to the convention center. He arrived alone, without his friend. He greeted his wife and immediately pulled her into a hug, then signaled for us to hurry and board the mail truck. He then took us across the Crescent City Connection [the bridge linking the West Bank to the East Bank of New Orleans], and drove to the ship, where they offered us a light snack and some cool, refreshing water. And that's when we called you, Monica. A few hours later, Vanessa and Angie arrived to pick us up, thank the Lord!

By dinnertime, Bernadine and Arthur had showered, changed clothes, and taken very long naps. Once they were awake and ready, Bernadine continued recounting the events of that day, but with added reflection and amazement. Bernadine continued:

Looking back, I can't help but wonder—was Nicole even real? Or was she an angel sent to deliver us? How else could she have reached her husband, who just happened to be across the river on a ship, when no phones were working? How had she come to the convention center alone, with no explanation, and why did she move through that chaos untouched? When her husband pulled up in that mail truck, there was no one else in sight but us; though every other time, crowds swarmed any vehicle for food, water, or escape. It was as if the world paused for us. Where did he even get the truck, or the keys? And how did we drive away unseen? I didn't think about it then, but now, every detail feels unearthly. She was beautiful, radiant almost; and yet no one stopped her. How was she able to reach him when even the satellites were down? None of it was possible, and yet it happened.

The family members looked around the room as if someone might finally put the puzzle together. Yet silence hung heavily. What had happened defied logic, and in that silence, the only thing left was wonder.

Bernadine turned to Arthur, and he responded in a straightforward tone, "It was the Lord's work."

Bernadine believed Nicole was an angel sent to save her and her husband. She insisted that, while they were at the convention center, she prayed nonstop; first with Arthur, then with Nicole, but mostly by herself.

I sat next to Bernadine as she gave her testimony. She held my hand tightly and declared, "This was my prayer. I prayed this all day, every day, since the arrival of the storm." She bowed her head, closed her eyes, and recited Psalm 23:

"The Lord is my Shepherd; I shall not want. He maketh me to lie down in green pastures: He leadeth me beside the still waters. He restoreth my soul: He leadeth me in the paths of righteousness for His name's sake." (Psalm 23:1-3)

As she finished her prayer, she lifted her head and opened her eyes, and this was the first time I saw any calmness on her pretty face. It was as if she were telling God that He had heard her prayers and responded to them. Bernadine was a strong woman of faith, convinced that, through prayer, God sent an angel, Nicole, to lead them to safe harbor. I asked Bernadine if she had gotten Nicole's phone number. She said, "Yes," but when she reached for the number in her purse pocket, it was not there.

By the time I woke up the next morning, the Morans had already left for Florida to visit their daughter. Monica told me Bernadine wanted to get as far away from Louisiana as possible, though she wanted to make sure Angie and I knew how much she and Arthur appreciated our picking them up.

It would be five years before I saw the Morans again. In June 2010, I went to visit my sister, Vicki, who still lived in New Orleans East. As I turned the corner to enter her street, I saw the Morans getting out of a yellow Cadillac in the driveway of a corner house. When I parked, I asked if they lived there, and they confirmed they did. For years, I had visited my sister without realizing that the Morans lived just ten houses away.

Of course, we hugged and acknowledged how happy we were to see each other. Bernadine invited me inside her tidy home, and we spoke briefly. I shared that I was planning to write a book about all the small miracles that happened during the days and weeks after Katrina. I told her I wanted to include their story in my book. She was very eager to talk with me because, as she said, the more she thought about everything that had happened, the more convinced she was that a higher power was responsible for their journey to safety. We agreed that once I started drafting the book, I would check with her and Arthur to ensure my details were correct.

Sadly, this wonderful couple is no longer with us. Mr. and Mrs. Moran both contracted Covid in 2020. Arthur died from the virus on March 26, 2020, and Bernadine joined him in the next life on April 1, 2020. Their family said they knew Bernadine would never have wanted to live without Arthur. Their love story lasted until the very end.

In my heart, we shared not one but two miracles. The first was that Angie and I were allowed by the state trooper to cross the guardrails to reach the Morans when no other non-commercial vehicles could. The second, of course, was Nicole and the incredible, unexplainable way the Morans were rescued by Nicole's husband from the chaos days before everyone else had been evacuated from the convention center and taken to safety.

And if, by chance, Nicole truly was an angel sent by God, I'd like to believe that Arthur, Bernadine, and Nicole have all reunited and given thanks not only to each other, but also to the higher power that answered Bernadine's prayers and provided them with their miraculous rescue.

# Chapter 6
## The Detour to the Family Reunion

In early September, just two days after helping the Morans, family members received another call for help from a distant cousin named Geraldine. This time, the call went to Monica's brother, Cordell, and his wife, Angie (who accompanied me to pick up the Morans). Geraldine's family included her, her husband, John, her son Derek, his wife, Angelique, and their three teenage sons, Chris, Quentin, and Justin. Despite Angie driving a Durango, the entire family couldn't fit into one vehicle, so Angie called and asked me to join the rescue team since I drove a Chevy Tahoe at the time. I could easily transport some of the group.

Geraldine's family originally planned to ride out the storm in a downtown hotel. However, on August 28, when management could no longer guarantee the safety of guests, they were asked to leave. With few options left, the family was forced to evacuate to the Superdome. Geraldine's son, Derek, who was deeply involved in the arts, carried his portable video camera, determined to document the unfolding crisis. He had already been in talks with a television producer about creating a documentary from his footage, one that would not only tell their story but also give Derek credit for capturing history in real time.

Geraldine's family was stranded at the Superdome with thousands of others, enduring unbearable conditions. When the floodwater finally receded downtown, contracted buses arrived to take the evacuees to safety. Families were told by the media they would be flown out of New Orleans, but no one knew their destination. Planes waited to carry them to Houston, Dallas, Phoenix, and other cities that had opened both their doors and their hearts. Fear and uncertainty hung heavily in the air. All anyone knew was that they were leaving behind devastation for an unfamiliar place, which was safe, until the day they could return home.

Geraldine's family had taken refuge at the airport along with hundreds of others desperate for a way out. Amid the chaos, her son somehow managed to reach a TV producer working on a documentary through reporters at the airport who had the means to connect with colleagues across the region. Unwilling to board a flight to an unknown destination, the family contacted Cordell, asking him to pick up her family and bring them to Belle Rose instead. The producer arranged for the family to leave the airport in a news van and head to the press staging area in Kenner, Louisiana, just fifteen miles from downtown New Orleans and a mere minute's drive from Louis Armstrong International Airport. Set at the corner of Veterans and Williams Boulevards, the staging area had become a hub for reporters and crews as they tried to coordinate coverage of the unfolding crisis.

Angela's husband, Cordell, offered to ride with us since we were traveling in the dark. A fortyish African American veteran, approximately 5'10", 230 lbs., with a muscular build, describes

Cordell at the time. He is a gentle giant and a gentleman, and he wanted to make sure that these two ladies returned home safely.

They received a call from Geraldine in the late afternoon, probably around 4:00 p.m., but we had to wait until Cordell finished work. So, we left Belle Rose at 7:00 p.m. The fifty-mile drive from Belle Rose to LaPlace, just outside Kenner, was smooth. I led in my emerald Tahoe, and Angie followed closely behind in her red Durango.

There were no vehicles on the road except ours. We were traveling in the dark, making the trip even more ominous than it had been when we picked up the Morans in daylight. We were approaching the Bonnet Carré Spillway, a 5.7-mile crossing that led directly to Kenner, our destination. We could see state troopers ahead, and we knew we would need to stop as we were driving non-commercial vehicles. I was ahead of Angela and Cordell, so when I saw the officer, I slowed to a complete stop and pressed the button to lower my window. I knew I had to appear as non-threatening as possible.

The public servant slowly approached my vehicle, cautious and direct. He was a tall, slim, African American officer in his mid-thirties, neither friendly nor hostile. With his flashlight in his right hand, he moved closer as I lowered my window to communicate.

Although I had not gotten a speeding ticket in many years (*no, seriously*), I knew what to do. I had already pulled my driver's license from my purse and the proof of insurance from the glove box. I handed both to the officer, and he accepted them but did not look at them very carefully.

In a rather authoritative tone, he asked, "Why are you on the road, ma'am?"

I began to explain who we were, why we were on the road that time of night, and what our destination was. I never knew I could talk so fast! It certainly was a mouthful.

"Umm, hello, officer. Well, if we can get through, we're heading to Williams Blvd. near the airport. The people in the vehicle behind me and I have a legitimate reason for being on this abandoned highway. We received a call from some family members, and they're currently outside the airport with reporters. We're going to pick them up. They were stranded in the Superdome, but were then picked up and taken to the airport. They told the people there that they didn't want to get on a plane but preferred to be picked up by family. So, we're the family coming from Donaldsonville to pick them up. It's a bunch of them, and that's why we needed two big cars. I promise you, we're coming straight back as soon as we get them. In about an hour, you'll see these same two vehicles on the other side of the road heading back home. May we pulleez get through?"

The officer started to chuckle.

At that moment, another officer from the second vehicle started walking toward my Tahoe. He was older, less muscular, and less fit than his younger counterpart.

"It's cool. I got this," the confident first officer said.

The other officer turned casually and went back to his vehicle. I didn't get the feeling that these men had ever met each other before this night's assignment.

I knew I had to let the officer know right away that I was harmless. I think it was my "pulleez" that made him chuckle. I'm sure he was thinking, "This story is so far-fetched it must be true." He motioned for me to keep going. Since my window was down, I signaled Cordell, who was driving the Durango, to continue. I started slowly, but I noticed Cordell wasn't behind me immediately and had stopped to talk to the officer, which made me even more anxious. We were cleared, and I was ready to move on. Thankfully, through my rear-view mirror, I saw the officer motion for them to go ahead, and that they were now catching up.

Once we passed the checkpoint, I stopped my vehicle on the empty highway, and Cordell followed suit. I asked him why he stopped, and he said he thought he had to, and he wasn't sure if the officer understood we were traveling together. I told him that if we approached other officers or barricades, I would definitely let them know we were together, so he could simply follow me.

We continued on I-10, and the darkness pressed in from every side. Usually, when crossing the Bonnet Carré Spillway, the headlights of other cars broke the blackness, giving at least some sense of company on the road. But this time there was nothing, no glow ahead, no glimmer behind. I'm not one to fear the dark, but this silence felt unnatural, almost suffocating. Each mile deepened the sense that we were utterly alone, moving through a void that had swallowed the world we knew.

As we exited the interstate and turned onto Williams Boulevard, just past the intersection with Veterans Boulevard, the staging area came into view. Floodlights blazed from every corner, casting stark illumination over an entire block. We pulled over and parked along Veterans, relieved to see people moving about. Entering the staging area was surprisingly simple: there were no guards, no credential checks, and no questions at all. The space was wide open, lined with tents, floodlights, cameras on tripods, and rows of tables and chairs, though activity was sparse. Thick electrical cords snaked across the ground, connecting equipment from tent to tent, and we stepped carefully to avoid tripping. No one stopped us, no one asked who we were or why we were there. It was as if our presence barely registered.

The journey through the press area transported me to another dimension. I had never seen a place that should have been bustling with people, noise, and laughter so quiet and subdued. Granted, the people in the staging area were working, but they were not laughing, directing, arguing, fussing, or showing any emotion. They all spoke in very low voices. These were TV producers, journalists, newscasters, and studio professionals. Still, we did not hear any conversations as we circled the complex looking for Geraldine and her family. I figured they were probably overwhelmed with this assignment. Hurricane Katrina broke records in destruction and human tragedy; reporting on it daily must have been very demoralizing.

I was very stressed out, now approaching five days after the storm. Not being able to go home to check on the damage to my own house weighed heavily on my heart. Not seeing my husband every day was hard on me. Not communicating with my sister or my brother was agonizing. Thinking about the three feral cats I fed daily and wondering about their fate haunted me.

The cell phone lines stayed down, and we could not communicate. We had no way to call Geraldine to find out where she and her family were. Had we gone through this trip, this long trip, for nothing? I felt my anxiety grow even more.

We circled the staging area repeatedly, but each pass yielded the same result—no family. I was sure we were in the right spot, yet the family was nowhere to be seen. Frustration crept in as confusion turned to desperation. "Where are these people?" A dull throb started at my temples, and I knew a migraine was about to come along for the ride.

We decided to split up and approach the area from both sides. Cordell and Angela went to the west side of the complex, while I headed toward the east. As I walked through this makeshift production studio under the stars, I saw two people standing outside one of the tents, so I asked them.

"Hello. Have you seen an African American family walking around here? The husband might be in a wheelchair or have crutches." I was unsure which was correct, but I knew he couldn't walk without assistance, as I had been told before leaving Belle Rose.

"No, ma'am. Sorry."

As I headed back toward the agreed-upon meeting spot, Cordell and Angela walked up to me with a well-dressed lady in her early sixties. Angela's voice was hesitant.

"Vanessa, this is Geraldine."

My manners vanished in an instant. "Hello," I said abruptly, then, without pause, blurted, "Where is the rest of your family?"

Geraldine's fear and frustration were unmistakable as she explained. "We were at the airport when Derek ran into his TV producer friend. He arranged for us to come here so y'all could pick us up. I stepped into the restroom at the airport, and when I came out, the rest of my family was gone."

I couldn't help but blurt out: "What do you mean they were gone? You just went to the bathroom, and when you got back, they just disappeared?" I should have been nicer, but stress and fatigue were overwhelming me.

Her voice rose in unwelcome excitement. "I think they put them on a plane! They were putting everybody on planes! They had us with a bunch of people, and I didn't even see the people that we were there talking to anymore; so, I think they put them on a plane with them."

By then, I was no longer the Southern Belle I was raised to be. Before I could say something very un-southerly, I cleared my throat.

"So, basically, we're bringing one person back to Belle Rose."

Angie and Cordell said nothing at this point. There really was nothing else they could say.

This was not anyone's fault. Not Geraldine's, not her family's, and not my road buddies'. It was just the whole damn situation, not just the family not being there, but everything else that came with this miserable life we were all forced into because of that cursed storm.

Geraldine broke the uncomfortable silence and begged, "Can we please just get out of here? I just want to leave this place."

"Are you SURE they're on a plane?" I pressed.

Her voice started to tremble. "Yes! Yes! Please, PLEASE take me away from here! This has been a terrible experience! They will call when they land, and I will join them later, but I just have to get out of here. Please don't make me stay another minute!"

Geraldine trembled as she clutched her purse, her shoulders hunched as if trying to shield herself. I had no doubt that, in normal times, she carried herself with strength, standing tall with her head held high in pride and confidence. But at this moment, the storm had taken that away. What stood before me was not weakness, but a woman exhausted by fear and uncertainty, doing everything she could just to hold herself together.

At that moment, I had no idea what Geraldine had gone through, but I could tell that whatever it was had left her deeply affected, to the point where she now believed her very life might be in danger. Cordell, Angela, and I stood there, frozen and silent for a moment because this was something none of us had experienced before. I could see they were trying to find the right words of comfort, as they needed comfort themselves. The night seemed never-ending, and instead of the reunion and positive outcome we had hoped for, we faced disappointment and disillusionment.

My heart was pounding as my thoughts spun in my head. We filled two large gas tanks and drove over 70 miles in the dark to pick up one person.

*Oh, Lord, please grant me the strength to stay silent.*

"All right, well, then let's go!" I turned to head toward the vehicles with the trio following suit.

I was furious as I walked back toward our two vehicles. Oh, my Lord, I was livid! Not at all at Geraldine. I felt compassion for her. I was not upset with Cordell or Angela. I was exhausted from this whole, terrible, rotten, God-forsaken Hurricane Katrina situation with every part of my being. It was clear that the devil was laughing because I was ready to cry. I began to pray silently.

*Dear Lord, please grant me the serenity to accept the things I cannot change, the courage to change the things I can, and the wisdom to know the difference.*

I kept going…

*It is nobody's fault. It's just one of those things! I can't change it, so I'll roll with it.*

Even with this weak attempt at a positive affirmation, I could not shake my anger. I kept thinking about gas shortages, driving a gas guzzler, and spending nearly two hours picking up one person. I said nothing until we reached the vehicles. I guess that Angela, Cordell, and Geraldine noticed my mood. They quickly announced that Geraldine would ride with them.

I said with no personality, "That's fine, just follow me out."

In my car, I gripped the steering wheel, as though it were a life preserver keeping me afloat in Katrina's swelling sea.

This affirmation I spoke aloud: "Vanessa, you need to calm down. Your heart was in the right place. Just put on some good music, relax, and enjoy the drive home. Do not let your nerves get the better of you. Chill!"

I began taking deep breaths, starting with quick ones, then slowing down for deeper ones. Then, I started my car and sharply turned the steering wheel to make a U-turn, waiting only to give Angela time to change her direction. The plan was to turn right onto Williams Blvd. and head west on Interstate 10.

At the southeast corner of the intersection stood the remnants of an Exxon station. As I eased forward, something unexpected happened. It was not that I heard a voice, but I felt a presence in the car beside me. A subtle, unseen hand seemed to guide my foot from the accelerator to the brake. I froze. I had two options: turn right toward home or go straight into the airport.

And then, somehow, I knew I was not supposed to go straight home. Under no circumstances was I to turn toward the interstate. I was meant to go straight. I remained there at the light, the seconds stretching into a full minute, before finally surrendering and acknowledging the voice within.

I activated my right turn signal and pulled into the empty gas station. Rolling down my window, I gestured for Angela, who had followed me into the station, to pull up beside me. Once our vehicles were side by side, Cordell lowered the front passenger-side window.

I calmly said, "I think we should go back and try to find them. For some reason, I do not believe they boarded a plane."

Geraldine, sitting in the back seat, lowered the second-row passenger side window to overhear my conversation with Cordell. She sat upright, turned her head toward the window, and exclaimed, "No, no, they are gone! I looked all over for them. I do not want to go back there. They are not there. I know it."

By then, I was eerily calm. The storm of anger that had raged inside me only minutes earlier had vanished, replaced by a sense of calm. It was not logic guiding me; it was a message, as clear as a voice in my ear. Almost in a whisper, I told her, "Geraldine, I think we should go. I cannot explain it, but something tells me they are still there. You do not even have to get out of the car if you don't want to; just describe them. We'll find them. You can stay in the car with the windows rolled up and the doors locked."

It was clear that Geraldine was processing my words. "I'm, I'm just not sure."

I asked intently, "Will you please trust me on this?"

Cordell and Angela sat quietly and very still, giving Geraldine her space to respond.

Something in my voice must have reassured her, and she nodded in agreement.

"If you really feel that we should go back, I will trust you. But I'm not getting out of the car. I just can't."

"I promise you won't have to do anything. We'll find them, okay?"

"Okay." She leaned back in the rear passenger seat and re-buckled her seatbelt.

I leaned in to lock eyes with Angie. "Angie, just follow me."

She nodded yes but said nothing.

We reversed both vehicles to re-enter Veterans Blvd. Instead of turning right to access the interstate, we drove straight through the intersection, continuing on Veterans Blvd. for less than a mile until reaching the road that leads directly into the airport. We were the only two vehicles on this straightaway, a rare sight at an airport as busy as Louis Armstrong's.

After driving along the winding road parallel to the runways, we reached the entrance of the airport near the parking lot. Two official vehicles with officers stood there, working together to keep order and prevent entry. I was the first vehicle to approach them. We had come this far. For the second time, I wondered if we had come all the way here only to be turned away. My lack of confidence was replaced by the faith that I held.

I stopped at the traffic signal just outside the parking area as a Jefferson Parish police officer approached my vehicle. He was of medium height, somewhat overweight, Caucasian, with thinning hair on top; he was pretty nondescript. He was holding a flashlight, and although it was on, he did not shine it in my direction. He spoke in an authoritative voice but was not rude.

"Ma'am, what are you up to here?"

Trying my best to come across as non-intimidating, I said, "Hello, officer, we are here to pick up some family members. The Durango behind me is with me as well. We are here to pick up an entire family that was stranded at the Superdome. They are here waiting for us. May we go in, please? Once we pick them up, we will be right out and heading back toward Baton Rouge."

He swung his flashlight toward the ground, then toward the parking lots, and motioned for me to proceed. No hesitation. No request for ID.

As I slowly drove away, on the grass near the fence to the right of our vehicles, I observed a relatively thin, short-haired, pearly-white domestic cat eating someone's leftovers from a Styrofoam container. I guess it was from one of the officers. I said out loud as if he could hear me, "Under other circumstances, little kitty cat, I'd be snatching your skinny little ass up and taking you home with me, but I have bigger fish to fry tonight." He kept munching, oblivious to my sentiments.

Angela did not stop to talk to the officers, following me into the airport parking lot instead. We drove into the short-term lot closest to the terminal entrance. We had our pick of every available parking spot, so I immediately chose two places very close to the terminal. As I turned into one of the stalls, Angela picked up on my cue and parked the Durango two spaces to the right. Even the usually busy parking lot's emptiness was an eerie sight. It felt as if we had driven into another dimension.

I was pleasantly surprised to discover that Geraldine was willing to leave the safety of the vehicle to find her family. Although hesitant, she understood we needed her to identify her family, so she bravely exited the SUV with Cordell and Angela.

I offered a word of caution. "Hey guys, leave everything in the car: purses, fanny packs, whatever. Just bring the car keys." I approached Geraldine, gently took her arm, and reassured her: "I'm proud of you! You're going to be fine. I promise."

She responded by hugging me and said, "I believe you, Vanessa."

Since I was the one who started this dance, I felt obligated to take the lead. I told the team, "Let me do the talking, alright?" By that point, I sensed that we would not only find this family but also overcome any obstacles between us and them. The way had already been paved for a family reunion.

We walked straight toward the first set of terminal doors, where another row of police cars was stationed. Two officers stood at the front of the lead vehicle, their posture heavy with exhaustion. Stepping a little ahead of the others, I approached one of the officers and asked, "Sir, we're here to pick up some family members. Where should we go?"

He squinted and asked, "How did you get in here? They're not supposed to let anyone in."

I said, "Well, sir, we entered through..."

Before I could finish, he said, "Just about everybody from tonight's pickups have all been put on planes, but if you want to see who's left, just walk that way." He pointed to the right outside the terminal.

After expressing my gratitude, I rejoined Angela, Cordell, and Geraldine, sharing the information from the police officer. We then began walking along the outside of the terminal toward the Southwest terminal area, where, pre-Katrina, people picked up arriving passengers.

Just then, five very tall, and I do mean tall, National Guard soldiers exited the terminal ahead of us. My eyes immediately locked onto their exceedingly large rifles. The guardsmen walked in unison, not marching but moving step by step, remarkably precise and incredibly intimidating.

Geraldine started hyperventilating. "That's why I didn't want to come back here! That's why! All those guns!"

I instructed Cordell, Angela, and Geraldine to slow down and said I would approach the guards. "Geraldine, you guys stay back, okay? I'm going to ask them where the passengers are. Just stay back."

Instead of walking up behind the soldiers, I moved well to the right and said in an unalarming voice, "Ummm, hellooooo? Excuse me? Hellooooo? Hi there?"

They didn't hear me at first because they were walking quickly with their long legs, so I sped up and tried again. I asked a little louder, "Ummm, hellooooo? Excuse me? Hellooooo?" This time, they heard me. The one on the far right stopped; the others took maybe three or four steps and then stopped as well.

"Yes, ma'am?" He was in his early twenties, and he was about to earn all my respect.

"Hello, sir, we're here to pick up some family members. Could you please tell us where we should go?"

The young man very politely said, with the sweetest Southern twang, "Ma'am, I'm not sure where y'all came from, but if your family is still here, they're going to be right up ahead in that crowd. Otherwise, everybody else has been put on a plane."

"Thank you so much," I said, then watched as he caught up with his fellow guardsmen and continued their assignment to maintain order, once again in unison.

As I looked toward the soon-to-be passengers, I noticed that at least two hundred stranded residents were standing in a sectioned-off area, waiting to be allowed into the airport. I found it strange that they were told to stand there instead of being allowed inside the terminal to sit down and relax while waiting to find out their next destination. My heart went out to them.

I quickly dismissed that thought and realized I needed to tell Geraldine, Angie, and Cordell what I had learned from the young guardsman. By then, I was already ahead of them. So, when I turned around, I didn't see them.

*Dear Lord, what now? Where on earth did THEY go?*

My first disturbing thought was that they had been detained; that, finally, our luck had run out, and they had been taken to some official office inside the terminal to face an interrogation for trespassing. Or, God forbid, they were being led to the large group of people and told they would be placed on a plane whether they wanted to or not. Panic had reared its ugly head, and my imagination was now in full negative overdrive!

But then, I heard, "Praise to the Lord Most High! Oh my God! Oh my God! Y'all are here! Oh my God! She was right! She was right!"

I immediately followed the sound of that voice to the other side of a large pillar in the ground transportation area, just outside of short-term parking.

And there they were! Geraldine's family. The family was here! I briskly walked toward them.

Geraldine grabbed me. "Oh my God, thank you, Vanessa! How did you know? How did you know?"

I answered barely above a whisper, "I cannot explain it. I just knew."

I give credit to that voice. That unfamiliar yet soothing voice I heard in the car. That presence, that gently moved my foot from the accelerator to the brake.

Geraldine, Cordell, and Angie were exchanging hugs. I could hear their sobs and words of praise to God for reuniting the family. For the first time in many days, I saw genuine happiness. It was as if the Prodigal Grandmother had returned, and it was a reason to celebrate. Watching the grandsons cling to their grandmother and seeing the relief on their faces was a touching sight. They knew that, somehow, some way, Geraldine would find her way back to them that night. They weren't going to leave without their beloved matriarch. Their faith guided them to step away from the eager crowd waiting to board planes to safety. And their faith proved true when they saw Geraldine walking toward them. Seeing the family's pure relief and happiness warmed my heart. As Justin, the youngest grandson, exclaimed, "Grandma, I knew you were coming back. I knew it!" I felt a heaven-sent joy. I wouldn't be driving home alone in that big Tahoe.

I experienced some divine intervention, and I was guided back to that airport. The family was there, waiting for us to arrive and pick them up, despite the odds. While the message came to me loud and clear, it also came to them. They were never going to leave that airport without Geraldine.

The family's brief relief at reuniting was short-lived. We were still in Kenner, it was past 10:30 p.m., and a two-hour drive home lay ahead. Every one of us was exhausted. What we had witnessed all night—the confusion, the tension, the uneasy presence of authority—was only a small part of the larger chaos unfolding in the Crescent City and across the storm-ravaged parishes. This was the grim reality: the city was flooded with fear, desperation, and weapons. *Two Tons of Guns*. I knew it was time to leave, and quickly.

Angie and I hurried back to the parking lot to bring the vehicles around for the family. It was the first moment we had all night with just the two of us, and our first chance to process what had just unfolded. As we walked, I caught her glance, my eyes wide with a mix of exhaustion and wonder. She finally broke the silence: "What a night."

"Oh my God, Angie! Can you believe this?"

Angie, with a look of awe, responded, "Girl, I have NO idea! I mean, I didn't think we would get past the first set of state troopers in LaPlace. And then, I just knew they were going to turn us around at the airport entrance."

I chimed in, still questioning. "How the heck did we get through? Not just the LaPlace guys, but the guys at the entrance, the two officers by the terminal, and the National Guardsmen? I mean, they all questioned how we got in here, but none of them told us to get out."

She then asked the question that had been on her mind. "And how did you know? How did you know they would be here? I mean, what made you insist that we come back to the airport?"

"I can't explain it. It wasn't like I heard a voice, but I guess you could say I received a message. And the message was that we needed to go back to the airport to find Geraldine's family."

Still amazed, Angie said, "Girl, this is all too much! It's like divine intervention!"

As Angie gave witness, I briefly stopped in my tracks with my hands raised in celebration. I paused to glance at the sky, and with gratitude expressed, "Lord, this is you! This is all you!"

The sky was clear, almost heavenly, with stars shining brighter than I could ever remember. Just hours earlier, while driving across the Bonnet Carré Spillway, I had been gripped by the suffocating darkness and fear. Now, standing under that vast canopy of light, the stark contrast between dread and wonder was overwhelming.

We settled the family between the two cars. My first priority was to get us out of the airport and onto Interstate 10, heading west. As we drove past the remaining evacuees toward the airport's exit, we came up on yet another Jefferson Parish police officer leaning against his vehicle. This officer raised his hand as a signal for me to stop.

I stopped, lowered my window, and before he could say anything, I calmly asked, "Hello, Officer. We just picked up some family members and are leaving. Should we exit the usual way out, like when the airport is normally open, or is there another exit we should take?"

This officer was not nearly as friendly or accommodating as any of the previous civil servants. He grumbled, "How did you get in here? They're not supposed to let anybody in here!"

I took a breath and respectfully responded, "Sir, when I told the officers at the entrance that we were picking up family..." but before I could finish to let him know that they let me in with no problem, he cut me off.

"Never mind, just leave. Do it like you normally do!"

In my mind, I responded with, *'Sure thing, Grumplestiltskin.'*

But aloud I politely said, "Yes, sir! Thank you!"

We exited the airport, entered Interstate 10, and, before long, every single exhausted passenger in the back seat was asleep. I told Geraldine, who was in the front passenger seat, that she was more than welcome to take a nap, and that I would listen to my music to keep me company. But she wanted to stay awake with me on our long drive to Belle Rose.

She told me the whole story about their experience in the Superdome. She described her son's dealings with the TV producer and the terrible experiences they faced, starting with the Superdome and ending with the mix-up at the airport. I felt a great deal of empathy for this close-knit family and everything they endured. The more Geraldine talked, the more I liked her. As we continued back to Belle Rose, she asked me why I was so determined to return to the airport.

"Geraldine, honestly, we were about to head home right then and there. But there was this force. I will never be able to explain it. It is like an unknown force gently moved my foot from the gas pedal to the brake pedal. It felt like everything was in slow motion. And I cannot say I heard a voice, but I did. I know it sounds unbelievable, but the words were clear: 'Go back to the airport.' And as upset as I was, and I know you could tell, this calmness suddenly took over me, and I knew that somehow I was doing the right thing by taking you back there to find your family."

Expressing heartfelt gratitude, joy, and relief, Geraldine declared, "Well, I'm so glad you did! God was truly with us!" She raised her hands in praise as she spoke those words.

I chimed in. "Yes, God has been around a lot lately! This is the second situation that Angie and I have been involved with this week, where we were able to accomplish something even when the odds were completely against us. It is almost like they are little miracles sent down from heaven or something."

This was the first (but not the last) time I vocalized the term "little miracles" out loud.

# Chapter 7

## My Promise to Black Cat

The highest compliment someone can give me is to call me a crazy cat lady. I adore my fur babies. I am the proud mom of three cats. I've taken in strays that have landed on my doorstep, the roof of my car, and the roof of my house. I've adopted cats given away from a Walmart grocery basket, and even a kitty who jumped into the front seat of my car in the CVS parking lot when I opened the door. (And yes, I always check for microchips—always!)

I was a Cat Mama to three little furballs at the time of the storm: Tinker, a white, short-haired, male domestic cat; Bootsie, a female Tuxedo; and Pumpkin, a tiger stray who showed up on our doorstep about a year before Katrina. Pumpkin, 100 percent deaf and 80 percent blind, was quite old and wanted to spend her last years with a family that provided food and shelter. My husband said the word on the streets in Cat World was that the lady at 11275 would take her in, and they were right!

Six months before Katrina, a silky and somewhat mysterious black kitty appeared on the walkway leading up to our front door. We had no idea where she came from, but there she was. I was already feeding two other ferals I named Grey Cat and Yellow Cat because of their markings, so I added Black Cat to my feeding routine. They all kept their distance and never let me pet them. They never tried to enter the house, preferring to stay away, knowing I would leave out food, let them eat, and come back later to scoop up and wash the small bowls I used for feeding them. Still, the black cat would often show up solo, turning onto her back in our walkway when my husband was outside washing the cars or cutting the grass. He never tried to pet her, but she seemed to find comfort in his presence.

One day, about a month or so before the storm, as I was sitting on the bench in front of my house reading, Black Cat appeared out of nowhere (as cats often do) and leaped onto my lap. I was stunned! She had never done that before. However, when I attempted to pet her, she growled at me. That called for a response.

"Well, excuse YOU! You hopped onto MY lap. I thought you wanted to be petted."

Then, I looked at those claws and thought, *"Aww, hell nah,"* because they were long and scary. Black Cat seriously needed a mani/pedi. When those claws dug into my jeans, I froze in place. So, I just sat there in detention for about fifteen minutes. I did not move. I did not speak. I did not breathe.

Eventually, my husband came looking for me. As he opened the door, I begged, "Baby, you've got to do something to get this cat off my lap!"

He had his keys in his hand. He aggressively jingled them, and Black Cat hopped off my lap and disappeared as quickly as she had appeared. He thought it was funny. I was not amused. She sat on my lap again another time, but this time I had my own keys with me. I did not chase her off at first because I wanted to make some progress with her. I figured this was her way of taking that first step. However, as soon as I moved my hand, those claws dug into my jeans again, and she growled.

"Little girl, you're kind of psycho. I think we're going to postpone this bonding thing for another time." I jiggled the keys, and off she went.

Fast forward to August 26. After finishing the house chores and taking pictures of our belongings for insurance records, I was ready to pack my SUV. One thing Louisianians know is how to pack for hurricanes. I made sure to store as many family photos as I could in a large container. Back then, we didn't have the luxury of storing thousands of photos on a 6" x 3" device called a smartphone. We had to pack the photos, displayed in ornate, glass-enclosed, silver or gold-plated frames, with the larger ones weighing several pounds. I also packed family keepsakes in this container, along with knick-knacks from around the house that held sentimental value.

A second container stored our important papers, jewelry, extra blankets, toiletries, cat blankets, and other travel essentials. Another container held canned food, a case of water, paper towels, and toilet paper. Included were a manual can opener, flashlights, and C and D batteries—essential before smartphones with built-in flashlights became common.

I would venture to say that if I had to pack for a hurricane today, I could manage with less than one full container. There are now blow-up pillows, shrink-wrapped blankets, smartphones for photos, documents in PDF format, and pre-moistened towelettes. But the toilet paper stays! There is no substitute for that.

When I opened the front door to deliver the first container to my Tahoe, I was surprised to find Black Cat sitting there waiting for me. She startled me with a loud, "Meow."

"Hey, there," I acknowledged. "I will feed you as soon as I get back inside the house."

But she wasn't interested in food. I learned that when I offered her a can of wet food. She ignored it and sat in her usual spot near the door.

"Alright, well, maybe you're not hungry. Okay, I've got to run, Black Cat."

She patiently sat there by the food, completely ignoring it. She watched me as I headed back into the house. At first, I didn't think much of it, thinking maybe she had snuck a bite somewhere else and was only looking for something specific from me. Unfortunately, this was not the best day to play the feline finicky card.

I went back into the house and grabbed the second container. I figured she would probably be gone, but no, she was still sitting there. This time, I ignored her and carried the second container down the walkway to the vehicle. This time, she walked with me and chatted the entire way.

"Meow, meow, meow, meow." I thought she was upset about my food choice and was trying to tell me she wanted something else. I obviously didn't understand the first message.

Black Cat stayed by the side of the vehicle the whole time I was working to carefully place the container into the back of the Tahoe. As I walked back to the house to get the third, she began talking and stalking again. "Meow, meow, meow, meow!" In her little mind, she was saying, "Miss Vanessa, can you take me with you? I will behave. I won't fight with your spoiled rotten, umm, I mean your indoor cats."

What we were experiencing was a communication breakdown.

I responded, "Black Cat, I gave you your favorite food; maybe you want some crunchies? Okay, I will get you some." Before bringing out the third container, I brought her a small bowl of dry cat food.

Once again, she looked at the bowl and just sat there. Well, by then, I needed to pick up speed; time was wasting. My three kitties, all neatly tucked in their individual travel cages inside the house, would be the last cargo to be added. Then I was heading toward the safety of Belle Rose, LA.

I grabbed the last container, and the same thing happened. Black Cat led me to the car, meowing as before, but louder and with more emotion.

Yes, cats do communicate their emotions. Ask any cat guardian.

I finally caught it. "Oh, my goodness, baby, you want to come with me? Honey, I can't bring you with me. I only have three cat carriers. You don't know my kitties. I've never picked you up, and, well, you're kind of feral."

I believe she understood that I was declining her request.

However, my negative response certainly went unheard.

As I brought Tinker out, Black Cat started meowing even louder and walked very close to my feet, so much that I had to watch my steps to avoid stepping or tripping over her. I began to feel emotional.

"Black Cat, I can't take you, baby. I'm sorry. I just can't. But I'll leave you plenty of food, and you'll be fine. I promise I'll be back in two days."

She knew something I didn't; that there was no way I would be back in two days or two weeks; it would probably be closer to two months. I then brought my Bootsie out, and the meows turned into cries for help. I burst into tears.

"Baby, I can't take you with us. I just can't. I wish I could."

I was crying because, first, I did not have a fourth pet carrier, and second, Black Cat did not know my cats. Trying to acclimate her and get her to share space with my babies would be a hurricane in itself. Pumpkin was older, deaf and blind. The fact is that if I took her, I would be exposing the family in Belle Rose to a borderline feral cat who could attack anyone at any time.

Black Cat again escorted me back and forth to drop off Bootsie and then finally Pumpkin. By then, I was an absolute wreck. I was fully aware that Black Cat knew I was leaving, understood she was on her own, sensed a storm was coming, and felt I was abandoning her. Emotions were intense, both hers and mine.

My final trip involved grabbing my purse and keys and making sure the front door was locked. It was as if Black Cat knew this was the final trip: she sat just to the left of the front door, watching me. I could feel her beautiful, yellow eyes piercing into the back of my body. I was crying so hard by then that I could barely see. As I started my vehicle, I made a promise I believed in my heart that I could keep. I stepped back out of the car and walked up to her.

"Black Cat, I'll be back in two days. I promise. Two days! And I'll give you a good treat when I return. And I'm going to work with you to make you a part of our family, because I think that's what you want, right? Now, eat your dinner. Two days, baby, two days. I promise."

However, I was not back in two or three days, or even two or three weeks. Because the levee broke, and our neighborhood was flooded with nearly four feet of standing water. We heard reports of the National Guard discovering dead animals all over the area. Those that weren't dead, mainly dogs, were now running in packs, desperately searching for food. Even dogs once kept as pets had become feral. My poor Black Cat. Why didn't I find a way to take her? I cried for days, overwhelmed with guilt and sorrow.

As an employee of the power company, my husband was considered a first responder and could enter any area where the water had subsided. He and some of his coworkers attempted to enter the eastern New Orleans area where we lived several times, but they had to turn back each time due to the high water. After several weeks, he was finally able to enter the area near our home. Every time he was able to make the seventy-five-minute trek to Belle Rose to see me, I would send him off with a care package of wet and dry cat food, bottled water, plastic spoons and bowls.

With a deep sense of guilt and desperation in my voice, I gave him specific instructions. "Promise me you will try to find her. Call her name; she knows her name. And if you don't see her, put that food out front where she used to eat so she will smell it. If she's there, she will come out to eat."

Those were my marching orders every time he went out there. Each time, when he returned to Entergy's base of operations, I would call him. "Did you see Black Cat? Did she come out?"

"No, I didn't see her," came his answer. "I called her name. I put the food out just like you said, but she didn't come out."

"Okay, what about Yellow Cat or Grey Cat? Did you see either one of them?"

"Vanessa, I did not see any cats or dogs. I don't think any pets left behind survived."

He was not trying to be mean-spirited; just realistic. I couldn't believe this strikingly beautiful, onyx creature had lost her life because I couldn't come up with a plan to take her with me. I grew more upset and tense as the weeks passed.

As the areas became safe to enter, Mayor Nagin allowed access to specific areas in New Orleans. He permitted residents in those neighborhoods to enter and evaluate the damage to their property. However, my neighborhood did not make the list. I was still denied access to my home, which meant I was unable to look for Black Cat myself. Agitated, I kept thinking, *If the water is down, why the hell can't we go out there when everyone else in the city can go into their neighborhoods and see their houses?*

The stress of all this was taking its toll on me. I was losing control of my eating habits, and I was regularly suffering from migraine headaches. My only relief came from two sources: migraine medication, which I didn't have, and my chiropractor, Dr. Kenneth Pace in Metairie, whom I hadn't seen in several weeks before the storm. My neck was causing me severe pain every day, and I needed an adjustment.

It was now Monday, September 27, 2005, a full month after the storm. I called Dr. Pace's office, expecting to hear a recorded message, hoping to find out when they would be back. I planned to leave a message, but when I dialed the number, Mrs. Pace answered.

Startled, I asked, "Hi, is the office open?"

She replied, "Yes, this is Kenneth's wife. And this is our first day back, and we are so excited."

"Hi, Mrs. Pace. Oh my goodness. So am I," I said with glee. "Any chance I can come in tomorrow?"

"Yes, ma'am, of course. Come anytime. We will be here all day." she answered.

So, the very next day, I drove the one hour and forty minutes to Metairie for an unofficial two o'clock appointment. My husband called as I was leaving Belle Rose, however, and asked me to swing by the Walgreens in Donaldsonville to pick up some film he had dropped off several days earlier. He had taken photos of our house and his parents' house when he first accessed those areas. I picked up the pictures but didn't take the time to look at them. I figured I would do so once I returned home from the chiropractor.

I arrived at Dr. Pace's office exactly at 2:00 p.m. Thankfully, only one other patient was there, so I was seen immediately. Relief was near. The office was quiet, and since I wasn't quite ready to get back on the road, we started talking about the entire terrible experience of Katrina. As I told Dr. Pace about what my husband witnessed as a first responder, I remembered I had the pictures in the car that he had taken. When I retrieved them, Dr. and Mrs. Pace and I looked through the images.

"Doc, I haven't even seen these pictures yet," I said.

Dr. Pace and his wife reviewed the photos first and then handed each to me after viewing. As we examined the photos of my in-laws' home, we noticed the house had not been securely bolted onto the pillars supporting it, which caused the structure to shift to the left and then settle at an almost 45° angle.

"Wow! That's something how they didn't secure the house to the pillars!" Dr. Pace expressed in disbelief.

"Yes! The house was renovated just a few years ago, and my in-laws were thrilled to be in it. But evidently, they did a shoddy job when they placed the foundation onto the pillars."

Dr. and Mrs.. Pace then started looking at the photos of our house. "So these are of your home?

"Yes," I practically mourned.

"You have a very nice place. I mean, you could tell it was a nice house before the storm," they said.

"Yes, it was beautiful. My husband kept the lawn meticulously manicured, and the pool was always spotless. I mean, there was never so much as a leaf in the water. And now, we have everything in there, except for the kitchen sink!"

As I said this, I realized my attempt at a joke was really my backhanded way of trying to accept what had happened to our beautiful home. It is said that humor heals pain, but in this case, there wasn't enough humor in the world to lighten the burden of this heartbreak.

Dr. Pace continued to look at the photos. Then he asked me, "Is this your cat?"

At first, I thought maybe it was a stray that Lamart took a photo of while scouting the neighborhood. However, when I looked, the last two pictures in the set were of Black Cat! Clearly, Lamart had captured these photos of Black Cat before the storm with his 35mm camera. When I saw those pictures, my emotions overflowed.

I started to cry in front of the Paces and said, "Yes, that's my cat."

To explain my tears, I told them my story and why I couldn't bring Black Cat with me. They were genuinely sympathetic. I told them I was going to find a way to go look for her. They wished me luck, but I think they thought I would do this at some point in the future. What they didn't know, and what I failed to tell them, was that, at that moment, I decided to look for her that day!

I first tried to enter I-10 East, heading toward my home, from Veterans Boulevard, a major road through Metairie that leads into Kenner. The entrance was blocked. I drove one mile eastward to the next exit, and there was also a barricade. Still, I was determined.

To this day, I still can't piece together how, or even where, I slipped onto the interstate. I only remember the shift from I-610 to I-10, steering east toward the familiar, though now strangely unfamiliar, streets of home. Maybe an officer had stepped away for coffee, or maybe, in the swirl of post-Katrina confusion, a gap in coverage opened just wide enough for me to pass through. My point of entry remains as blurred now as the letters on my last eye exam chart.

As I held the monopoly on the interstate, it felt like I was in a Twilight Zone episode. Moments after I transitioned from I-610 to I-10, my vehicle reached the highest point of the interstate, affectionately called the "High Rise" - the gateway to New Orleans East. Below me, the city lay quiet and heavy. As I descended, I saw train cars on their sides, scattered across the tracks below, like broken toys. They looked so small from above, reminding me of my brother Tony's Lionel Train Set that we played with as kids. Those innocent memories hit me like a locomotive, and that's when tears started to flow, staying with me all the way to the Lake Bullard exit, my destination.

This was the eeriest drive I had ever taken through the aftermath of Katrina. I felt completely isolated and scared but stayed determined. At each exit I passed, the ramps were sealed off with police cruisers, state troopers, national guard, military and other government vehicles, barring entry, like sentries during the night. Each barricade was a stark reminder that life as I once knew it was sealed off; there was no going back, no matter which exit I chose. The orders for all residents to turn around carried a heavier message, that our past lives were no longer accessible, and the only path forward was through detours that led into uncertain futures.

I was trembling. Reality had set in.

"Vanessa, what the hell are you doing?" I scolded myself. "You're seriously going to get arrested."

I didn't care. I couldn't stop.

I passed each exit with the weight of knowing that, at any minute, flashing lights could appear in my rearview and I would be arrested. Still, I pressed on, scanning for Bullard Avenue. When I finally reached my turnoff, my pulse quickened. This was the moment of truth. They would ask how I'd gotten there and why I had not turned back. I had no excuse. No lies. Only the truth. Which meant I was ready to face jail.

There were two police cars at the exit. A blue-and-white, older police car was parked closest to the exit, while the other police vehicle was at the very end of the exit on Bullard Avenue. That patrol car was black and white. My panic rose as I came to a complete stop at the first vehicle. The lone police officer walked toward my Tahoe. He was about 5' 7", in his mid to late thirties, and of Latino descent. He motioned for me to roll down my window. I complied without hesitation. I expected to be led away in handcuffs.

Before he could say anything, tears in my eyes, I took the lead. "Officer, I know I'm not supposed to be here. I know I'm breaking the law. I know you could arrest me. But, I'm really, really worried about my cat. I had to leave her, and I'm so worried about her."

His demeanor was especially calm. No handcuffs, no pointed finger, no scolding. He was so kind. In a gentle voice, he said, "Lady, I am not supposed to let anyone enter this neighborhood, but I am going to let you in. Go get your cat. Go straight to your house, pick up your cat, and head back to where you came from. Do not drive around. The National Guard will be here soon, and if they see you, they will mistake you for a looter. They will not ask questions. They will arrest you on the spot. So don't be long. You hurry up, alright?"

Between tears, I said, "Yes, Sir! I promise. I will find her and get back on the interstate right away. Thank you SO much!" I smiled at him, sniffed back some more tears, and said, "God bless you!"

He smiled, tapped the side of the car, and sent me on my way. Neither of us mentioned the tall African American officer standing outside the black-and-white police car at the far entrance of the exit.

As I pulled away and headed toward the second vehicle, that officer didn't even look in my direction. As I eased past the second vehicle, the officer remained indifferent, leaning against his car with the ease of someone waiting for a bus rather than guarding a broken city. I held back every emotion I had, and once I passed him, I burst into wild laughter but with tears streaming down my face. It was the sound of release, of a dam inside me breaking wide open, carrying grief, fear, panic, and relief in its current.

"Oh my God, oh my God, oh my God! I got through! He let me through. Holy crap! I did it!" I thanked God, Jesus, and my grandmother, in that order. "Oh my God, thank you! Jesus, thank you! Mama, thank you!"

My joy was short-lived. As I veered right onto Bullard Avenue, a stark reality hit me. I had grown so used to the avenue's brilliant colors: the royal blue of the Exxon sign to the right; the bright, golden-yellow Shell sign to the left; the bold red-and-white Kentucky Fried Chicken sign down the way, mirrored by the soft tan-and-blue of the Taco Bell next door. That kaleidoscope of daily life was gone. Where did all the beautiful, green foliage on the neutral ground go? In its place stretched nothing but a suffocating beige, as though the world had been drained of color, leaving behind a lifeless desert landscape. Branches and debris were scattered across the streets in an apocalyptic muddle, leading from the interstate to Fernley Drive, which was about five long blocks ahead. I drove carefully, navigating as if in a maze, making several sharp rights and quick lefts to avoid the branches strewn across the road.

How could we ever recover from this? My tears were like a leaky faucet; I could not turn them off. It was impossible to stop them. As if this wasn't bad enough, I turned onto my street and cried even harder. The colors of those gorgeous homes were washed out, faded, and ugly. All foliage, every carefully cared-for front lawn, was brown, stiff, and dead. I did not see any signs of life or vibrancy. Certainly, no sight or sounds of humans, dogs, or cats; not the beautiful chirping of a single bird. This land was barren.

I could only think about being responsible for that beautiful, precious cat not surviving this level of destruction. She knew. She kept trying to tell me that she understood this storm was going to be deadly, a killer, and that it was going to take many of God's creatures in the aftermath.

When I pulled into the driveway, my heart sank. A section of the roof was gone, torn away as if it were paper. On the white garage door, the mark of the National Guard told the world no dead bodies were inside. My beautiful home stood battered, scarred by Katrina's wrath, no longer the safe haven it had once been.

I stepped out of my car and faced the house, tears continuing to flow. Knowing the chaos that had happened just a few weeks earlier, I sobbed for Black Cat, convinced that she might be gone forever. I knew my petite, ebony, golden-eyed princess couldn't have survived the winds, the storm surge, the flooding, and the diseases the water carried into our once beautiful neighborhood. Still, I had come to rescue her, and I was not going to turn away or give up without pleading for my baby to appear. I remembered the police officer's words. He did not say, "Go look for your cat." He specifically instructed me to "Go pick up your cat," as if he knew she was there waiting for me.

I began to call for her.

"Black Cat? Black Cat? If you can hear me, please come out." I wasn't sure if I was speaking or singing. My only goal was to coax her out using the language and tone she recognized as my voice during feeding time pre-Katrina.

Nothing.

"Black Cat? Black Cat? Where are you, baby? Mommy's here to get you."

I looked around desperately, scanning for the slightest flicker of life. By the front door sat the bag of dry cat food Lamart had left behind, untouched. Not a single animal had clawed at it, not even in hunger. The sight turned my stomach. A wave of dread tightened my chest, and I called out again—this time, panic breaking through my voice.

"Black Cat? Black Cat? Baby, where are you?"

Nothing.

"Come on, sweetheart, I've come a long way to get you. I can't stay for long. Please come out. Black Cat?"

Then, as I stood there before my home, tears streaming like endless raindrops, a sound broke through the silence; so melodic, so precious, I was certain it had drifted down from the heavens.

"Meow."

I froze in place, startled. "Did I hear what I think I just heard? My next call for her was more of a whimper.

"Black Cat?"

"Meow!"

Good Lord! Was I hearing things now? Was my guilt so deep that I was imagining hearing her?

"Black Cat?" By then, my voice had jumped two octaves.

"Meow!"

It sounded as if she was calling from behind me, so I turned around, eyes searching frantically. I did not see her, but moments later, amidst the colorless sand, branches, and debris from Mrs. Johnson's driveway across the street, I saw a moving contrast; a gorgeous, ebony kitty with yellow eyes coming toward me. It was my Black Cat!

I repeated it. "Black Cat? Oh! My! God!"

She glided across the street toward me, in slow motion, each delicate paw striking the pavement with the crisp precision of a figure skater kissing the ice.

I remained rooted to the spot, unsure of her first move once she approached my space. She sashayed around me, as I stood motionless, not out of fear, but total shock, as she began rubbing the backs of my legs with her beautiful, little body. I didn't move for a long minute, letting Black Cat take the lead in this dance. Then she did what she had done before I left; she sat down next to me.

She was so calm. It was as if she knew that I would keep my promise to come back, and she had the patience of a saint. She did not come out when Lamart called for her, because he hadn't promised to come back for her. I did. And it was my voice that she expected. She waited, ever so patiently, for my return. And now I was here to fulfill my promise.

I cautiously stepped over to hood of the car, where I had placed a can of food, opened it and placed the food in one of the empty bowls my husband had previously left. I also opened a bottle of water I had in the car and poured some into another bowl. I set both in front of her. I was sure she would be starving and would devour the food, but she didn't. She ate very little and then resumed rubbing the backs of my legs.

The promise I had made to the officer echoed in my mind. We had to leave, and fast. The National Guard would be carrying out their orders to arrest anyone who dared to enter this forsaken area. I swung open the back passenger door of the Tahoe, its seats already folded flat like a cradle waiting in silence. With careful urgency, I gathered my baby into my arms and laid her gently in the back, her small body nestled safely against the upholstery. I closed the door with a quiet finality, sealing us into motion. I sat her right in the middle so I could check on her now and then during the drive to Belle Rose. I had never picked her up before, but today was the day she was coming home! If I ended up with scratches, so be it. But no: no bites, no scratches, no hissing. She allowed me to pick her up, and once I set her in the back of the car, she settled in. She sat back there so calmly. She tucked her little paws in and did not move, meow, or make a sound one time during the entire hour and forty-five-minute drive back to Belle Rose.

I, on the other hand, talked a hole in her head, telling her how sorry I was, how much I missed her, and how I would never, ever leave her again under any circumstances. I thanked God over and over for saving my little fur baby, and for providing me the determination and insanity to go and get her. I told her the entire story, starting back to when she escorted me on the many trips to fill the Tahoe just days before the storm. I explained to her why I could not take her, reminding her of the little incidents on the bench. On occasion, I would peek back behind me and observe her merely sitting there, paws tucked in, knowing that she was finally getting what she had requested weeks ago, to be saved, rescued, and claimed.

As I recited to her the events that led up to her rescue, I reverted to the term I used with Geraldine, this was a little miracle! How was it that the same roll of film Lamart used to take photos of the two destroyed homes also contained two pictures of Black Cat? And how was it that I just happened to pick up those photos on that morning and have them in the car? Had Dr. Pace not inquired about our home, and had I not remembered that the photos were in the truck, I might never have gotten the message that I needed to go and rescue her. To this day, I honestly do not know, or cannot remember, how I entered the interstate to head to New Orleans East in search of her.

Plus, how was it that when Lamart went out there on several occasions, bringing food with him and calling her name, she did not respond and show herself to him? Why did the first cop at the Bullard exit kindly let me access my neighborhood, and why didn't that second cop at the exit ask me anything? Most importantly, how did my baby girl survive all those weeks with no food, with all that murky water, and through winds that could have easily blown her clear across town to God knows where?

The news of Black Cat's rescue traveled quickly through the family upon my return to Belle Rose. Everyone knew that I had arrived in Belle Rose with three cats, and now I had four. They knew that I had left the house that day with no cats and returned with one. No one could believe that I had gotten through and managed to get all the way to New Orleans East and come home with yet another feline.

That first evening, though, I shared her full story with the entire family. Some of our cousins lived off the same exit in New Orleans, and because of my good fortune in getting through, they announced they would be going to New Orleans the following day. Hopefully, they reasoned, they would be able to take a quick trip to see the condition of their home. They went hoping to catch the same officer who let me through. Interestingly, they were turned around immediately and instructed to leave the area. We discussed the officer who had allowed me entry to the neighborhood upon their return, but they did not see anyone matching that officer's description. Could he have been an angel? Or was he simply a nice police officer whose heart was melted by a woman crying to get her fur baby?

One thing really struck me that evening. The officer never said, "Go look for your cat, Lady." He said, "Go GET your cat," as if it were a done deal. With all of the reports on the deceased animals found in that area, all these weeks later, how on earth did he know that I would find her?

I am convinced there is a much higher power at work here: first, with the Morans, then with Geraldine's family, and then with Black Cat.

When we returned home to Belle Rose, I gave Black Cat her own room so she could gradually get used to her new siblings. That night, I shared the bed in which she had found comfort. She allowed me to stroke her soft, silky black fur – a first! She nuzzled up under me and slept peacefully. Tears welled in my eyes yet again because I knew in that moment, she felt safe, secure, and—most importantly—that she understood why I had to leave her, and that she had forgiven me. As I lay with my precious black cat, I realized there had been blessings all along my sojourn to find and bring my baby to safety. I prayed for a miracle. But standing amid such damage and destruction, I believed there was no miracle left to be had; that is, until I heard it, the miracle of the meow.

Perhaps after everything she had endured, or simply because she finally felt safe, she chose to trust me. She sensed that the other kitties, the "spoiled ones," as she had first nicknamed them, meant her no harm. When we moved into our permanent home, I officially adopted her. From that moment on, she was no longer just Black Cat; she became part of our family: an indoor princess with yearly vet visits, daily feasts of wet and dry food, her own bed, a bounty of toys, and a Mama just crazy enough to risk jail time to come and rescue her.

Of all the little miracles, this one touched me the most. It was the hardest to relive while writing this book because of the emotions it stirs in me, as a fierce cat lover and a woman with strong maternal instincts. I do not know how many of her nine lives Black Cat used during and after the storm, but she was my miracle fur baby. For eleven sweet years, I cherished her as a content, indoor lap cat. My baby passed away in January of 2016.

*Her miracle was believing I would come back. Mine was that I did.*

# Chapter 8

## Miss Erma's Planted Message

Three days after the storm, residents of certain sections of Orleans and Jefferson Parishes could enter their homes and collect whatever personal items they could find. Access to the city was based on where the water first drained. We lived in the eastern section of New Orleans East, where much of the flooding occurred and remained well after other sections of the city were cleared for re-entry.

Finally, several weeks following Katrina's departure, we received authorization to return to our neighborhood. As I mentioned, my husband worked for the power company's storm duty team, so he had access to all areas of the city, including New Orleans East. However, he decided to wait until I could accompany him to enter our house. Though I had already seen the outside days earlier when I sneaked in to rescue Black Cat, I had not seen my home's interior since that was not the goal of that expedition.

On the journey to the house from Belle Rose, Lamart and I did not joke much, which was unusual. Usually, we found all sorts of things to laugh about when traveling together, but we were both clearly apprehensive about what storm damage to expect.

I began the conversation. "So, I saw that part of the roof was missing. Guessing it rained a lot in the house, huh?"

He responded, "Probably. But the majority of the water in the houses came from the levee breaking, not the rain." He continued, "Even though our house sits high, I could see the water line on the garage door. We got at least four feet of water, if not more."

I reflected on the personal items I kept on the first floor of this house. My grandmother on my father's side raised my sister, brother, and me after my mom died. I was just twenty months old, so my grandmother was the only mother I had ever known. I thought about the cedar chest I had inherited from her.

"I'm hoping that we can salvage Mama's cedar chest," I said with as much optimism as I could muster. "Maybe we can dry it out and it will be fine."

Although hopeful, I was not confident. Mama's cedar chest was decades old, and it had been in my grandmother's house for as long as I can remember. It was one of those beautiful, rounded Lane chests that had that distinct smell of cedar each time you opened it. On my thirteenth birthday, I asked my grandmother point-blank, "Ma, can I have that chest when I get older?"

"Nessa, you really want that chest?" she clarified.

"Yeah, Ma, it's going to be like my hope chest, like they show in the movies."

Mama responded positively, "If you really want it, you can have it. Your grandfather bought me that when we got married."

In that chest, Mama kept the nice keepsakes that my grandfather, had bought her when he was a merchant seaman, traveling to China, Japan, and all across the Orient. Over the years, those items were stolen in several break-ins, but the chest remained. Eventually, I arranged for the cedar chest to be shipped to me when I lived in California, and when I returned to New Orleans in 1997, the chest came home with me. It was one of two prized possessions I had courtesy of my grandmother.

The other was a queen-sized blanket that my grandmother crocheted as a gift for my sixteenth birthday. She asked me what I wanted, and when I told her I wanted a crocheted blanket, she was a bit shocked. I think she was expecting me to ask for something a typical teenager would ask for, like jewelry; but no, I wanted a crocheted blanket. It took her several months to finish, but it was well worth the wait. It is simply stunning. The intricacies and the handwork and the love my grandmother placed into that blanket do not compare to any other material item I have ever owned.

And by the grace of God, when I packed to evacuate the house, you can be sure that the crocheted blanket was at the top of the list; it was one of the first items I brought to my Tahoe. I have Mama's crocheted blanket to this day, and if ever I must leave where I live again, it leaves with me.

As we drove, I reflected that my husband, our four kitties, and I were safe, and that this was more important than any household item. All that could be replaced.

As we turned onto Fernley Drive, Lamart asked, "Are you ready for this?"

I replied quickly, "Yep. No time like the present."

Approaching the house, I experienced an instant headache. I'm not sure if it was from the stench of the water that permeated through the entire area or the knowledge that the damage was far worse than I'd even imagined. The one positive thing I could say was that, by following Ray's advice, every single board I had put up to protect our windows was still intact. Every one of them! That brought me about thirty seconds of joy.

My first observation was that our custom-built brick mailbox had been reduced to rubble, scattered about like a child's building blocks. We gingerly walked up the pebbled walkway, observing that our beautiful garden was a mess of uprooted shrubs, wilted blooms, and mulch scattered like confetti after a Macy's day parade. The massive sego palms that adorned the front of the house had died a slow and painful death, their branches now brittle and faded, slumped over like tired shoulders after a long fight. We approached the front door, and the muck was visible. Now, my husband is a strong man, but after many attempts at pushing the front door open, we were unable to get through.

"Let's go in through the back," I suggested.

Lamart agreed. "Yeah, because I don't know what's in front of that door, but whatever it is, it's not budging."

As we stepped through the narrow opening, the backyard came into view; and with it, a quiet heaviness settled over me. It wasn't just the physical wreckage that struck me, but the memories tied to every corner of that space. The grill where Lamart prided himself on his barbecue skills, the luscious banana tree in the corner near the deep side of the pool, the flower beds he'd planted one spring afternoon when everything felt full of promise. Now, it all looked foreign. Familiar shapes were buried under debris, colors dulled by mud and water, the stench drowning out the scent of the methodically planted jasmines.

I realized then that the damage was not just to the house, it was to the life we'd built around it. And yet, standing there, I also felt a strange sense of clarity. We were still here. Still together. And maybe that was enough to start again.

We had installed an inground pool several years earlier, and my husband kept that pool meticulously clean. We had an automatic pool cleaner on a timer, so the pool was always ready for a quick swim, even when guests unexpectedly arrived.

I had never seen the pool in such a deplorable condition. It was heartbreaking, knowing we had gone to great lengths to keep it clean. The first things we noticed were two pieces of fence in the pool. The water was thick and muddy from the dirt and sand Katrina had blown in. That beautiful banana tree, once providing a tropical feel to the backyard, was now uprooted and tossed into the water like a beach ball, sharing the pool with tree limbs, debris, and our neighbor's cable dish.

Our pool was, as Niecy Nash would say on the HGTV show, *Clean House*, a hot mess!

Dirt and debris covered the once salmon-colored pool deck, and our beautiful copper frog, proudly placed at the deep end of the pool, was dirty and coated with mud. I never had a chance to clean him because looters took him within days of our visit.

Lamart stood there, doing a full 360° inspection of the yard. While he managed the pool himself, he had recently hired a landscaper to plant perennials for a spring-filled garden and to ensure the grass was always cut neatly with hedges trimmed carefully. He looked around at the fence, which was partially tossed into the pool like a Nerf ball, and was speechless. This had been his home for nearly twenty years. I had only been there for eight, and I knew the pain I was feeling. I could only imagine his dismay and disappointment as he looked at the muddle that was once his beautiful home.

It was time to enter the house. Once again, Lamart struggled. After a few minutes of locking, unlocking, pushing, and pulling the door that led from the backyard to the great room, we finally gained access. There was no electricity, of course, but since all the blinds had been destroyed and part of the roof had blown off, plenty of light was coming in.

We had to navigate through the damp and musty floors in the great room to reach the kitchen. The smell hit us first: a crusty, mildewy, unsanitary, toxic odor. I had never smelled anything like it before, and I immediately felt dirty. More than dirty, filthy. Lamart and I both wore our large, ugly, black rubber boots, and our pants were tucked inside them, so I didn't feel dirty from stepping into anything other than toxic air. We both had thick gloves on and wore KN-95 masks, which was difficult for me because of my tendency toward claustrophobia.

We just stood there for a minute, trying to absorb everything we were seeing.

"Oh, dear God!" That was all I could say.

Lamart simply answered, "Damn."

Only weeks earlier, we sat in our great room on our exquisite, emerald-green couch, watching television with Tinker and Bootsie curled on my lap and Pumpkin in a fuzzy, round cat bed on the floor. I sat with my legs stretched out, while Lamart lay across the couch, fighting for lap space with the kitties. We understood, without saying a word, that the couch was no longer ours, but Katrina's. Its cushions, once soft and familiar, were soaked through with murky water and streaked with grime. It sat there like a ghost of holidays past, ruined beyond repair. That was when I looked at the white-washed coffee table with its glass top and saw the photo albums on its lower shelf. I realized I hadn't picked up the albums with the histories of the Despenza and Buggage families. I reached for one, my fingers trembling, and tried to pry it open, but the pages were fused together, swollen and sealed shut by water and time. The stench of the albums was worse than the overall house smell, so I just set it back down and headed to the kitchen, where Lamart had already entered.

Almost in a whisper, I barely heard Lamart call for me. "Come see." As I got closer, the tone of his voice made much more sense. "Can you believe this?" he continued, shocked. "Look at this. How did the refrigerator land on its back?"

Our kitchen was a galley kitchen and quite small. We would have expected this gigantic side-by-side refrigerator/freezer to have fallen face front, yet here it was on its back with both doors wide open. Because we learned of Katrina's direction only a few days before her arrival, I did not have time to empty the refrigerator, so it was stuffed. Imagine the smell of rotted chicken breasts, pork chops, broccoli, cooked red beans, and about three containers of Blue Bell Tin Roof ice cream (which they should bring back - just saying!). That was a totally different type of stench, almost bloody.

Every step felt like another step into hell. As we looked around the rest of our tiny kitchen, I saw that my beautiful wood canisters were ruined. The toaster and all other counter appliances were knocked over on their sides. However, just six inches above, there was a second counter, and everything on it was completely intact. We estimated that nearly 38 inches of water had surged through our home. Across the street, our neighbors weren't as fortunate. They fared even worse than we did, if that's possible. What spared us, if you could call it that, was a subtle rise in elevation on our side of the street. Just a few inches of grade made all the difference between devastation and total ruin.

We continued from the kitchen to the guest bathroom. The shower curtain was moldy and muddy, as were the floors. That bathroom had the most beautiful emerald green tile, but we couldn't see it because of the mud. I almost slipped as I entered, and Lamart had to grab my arm. "Vanessa, be careful," he warned with concern.

I exited the bathroom in reverse, holding his arm for dear life, and led him to the guest bedroom. There it was, my beautiful Lane cedar chest, broken into two pieces. Somehow, the top had come loose from the base. The inside was mildewed, streaked with layers of mud. I froze in my tracks, tears streaming down my face, overwhelmed by the harsh reality that this cherished possession was now lost forever. I felt angry at myself because, just before leaving, I thought about lifting the chest and putting it on the bed. But, since I never had much upper-body strength, I decided against it. Had I done that, might it have been saved? I will never know.

I looked at the small workout room and thought, *"Well, this can all be replaced."*

I opened the closet door that stretched along the wall, and my heart sank. My entire wardrobe, everything I had carefully chosen, worn, and loved, was destroyed. Clothes hung limp, smelly, and stained; shoes from my favorite designer (*Pancaldi*) floated in muddy water. Purses and scarves were crumpled, shredded, and unrecognizable. It was all gone, not just ruined but erased, as if the storm had reached in and taken pieces of my identity with it. This was the second time I lost an entire wardrobe. (*The first was in a fire in California in 1996.*) Again, these were replaceable, material items, but considering how hard I worked over the years to pay for them, it was a loss, no doubt about it.

We went upstairs to the main bedroom. The bedroom set, located well away from the French doors leading out to the small deck overlooking the pool, was in good shape: no water damage, no movement. We could have collapsed onto that bed and drifted into sleep from sheer exhaustion, but for the stench of mildew and the invisible threat of disease clinging to every surface. The main bathroom items were perfectly intact, as though the storm had merely whispered past instead of roaring through like a cyclone. Lamart's closet, near the French doors, was completely intact; the sliding mirror doors hadn't moved, and all his clothes, including his Air Force uniform and flight suits, were in perfect condition.

However, the tan recliner I moved to block the French doors, which opened inward, was on its side and about three feet away from the doors. The doors themselves had swung completely off their brackets and into the pool. I peeked my head out of that open space and looked directly into the pool from an overhead angle. I had a 180° view of the entire backyard, a yard that had hosted many pool parties over the years, where both his family and mine would gather for hours of eating, drinking, socializing, dancing, and celebrating life. The yard now stood as a silent memorial to the lives Katrina had claimed; some whose stories we'd seen on the news, and countless others still waiting to be found.

At this point, I could no longer hold back my tears, my heart heavy with pain.

Lamart noticed when I looked away and asked, "Vanessa, you okay?"

I replied, "No, not really. I mean, are you?"

"Not really," he acknowledged. But, being the eternal optimist, he offered words he hoped would calm me. "Vanessa, it's just stuff. And stuff is replaceable."

I retorted, "Not everything. Not my grandmother's chest!"

I think he realized at this point it was probably best to stay silent because I was caught up in my feelings, and logic was the last thing I wanted to hear.

We went into the walk-in attic, and it was as if time had stopped. Nothing was out of place. The shutters on the small window were intact. Everything in the attic was 100 percent salvageable.

There was only one other place to check, which was the garage. We already knew we couldn't open the garage door from the outside. This meant we had to squeeze past that disgusting refrigerator to reach the door leading out to the garage.

Returning downstairs, we checked the built-ins in the great room. This was Lamart's moment of truth. He had a collection of over 300 music albums that he started collecting in high school. They were now destroyed, victims of the flooding. He had a stereo setup that included a reel-to-reel system, a phonograph, a stereo receiver, a double cassette deck, and a 300-disc CD player, along with three-foot floor speakers and smaller Bose surround-sound speakers installed in the ceiling of the great room and billiard room.

(Watching any Star Trek movie was an incredible experience.) The system sat on the left side of the room, directly beneath the gaping wound in the roof. Everything below lay in ruin. This was American Pie, where the music died.

Lamart stood there for a long minute. "Man, my albums. You know how long I've been collecting these? I bought some of these at Eddie's Three-Way Record Shop back in the 60s."

Eddie's Three Way was the Crescent City's version of Tower Records. It had been a local record store not much bigger than a broom closet, but Lord, it had wall-to-wall albums, 45s, posters, and anything else you needed to have a bitching music collection back in the day.

Lamart sighed and then moved with me toward the dining room. The table and chair legs were covered in mud, and many items from the curio cabinet were displaced and broken, having fallen on the floor. Before evacuating, I moved all our tabletop plants from the first-floor rooms to the dining room table. Our house had many windows on the first floor, providing plenty of sunlight for nature's greenery to absorb and bloom as they pleased. When I boarded the house, the sunlight they could have enjoyed after the storm was completely blocked; remember, we believed we would only be gone for two or three days at most. We expected to return to slightly wilted plants; thirsty, sun-starved, but salvageable. Especially my beloved Ficus. Instead, what greeted us was the silence of the table crowded with lifeless stems, stripped of leaves, flowers, and any hint of revival. My temporary botanical garden had vanished.

We realized then we had done all we could that day.

Lamart asked, "You ready?"

I was and I wasn't. I wanted to grab every cleaning tool I could find and scrub that house from top to bottom! I wanted to turn back time and undo all the devastating damage Hurricane Katrina had done. I wanted to close my eyes and reopen them, only to realize that this nightmare was just a bad dream. I wanted Katrina to manifest as a human so I could beat the ever-loving crap out of her!

But, alas, I couldn't do any of that. There was nothing left to do but leave.

"Yup," I responded in tears. "This is depressing. Let's go."

We knew we would have to start over, make many repairs, and pray for patience and peace. I headed to the door that we used to enter the house, not wanting to turn back, as Lot's wife did at Sodom and Gomorrah. I feared that looking back would make me physically ill, though the sickness had already settled in my chest. I was heartsick. But I looked back anyway.

*And there it was!*

This one plant. This one fabulous, beautiful, blooming and thriving plant! Not just surviving but flourishing! How had I missed it when I was right there at the table? The plant looked lively, with stems and leaves standing upright, ready to be displayed. This plant was given to Lamart in January, eight months before, at his mother's funeral service. I had named the plant "Erma" after her, Mrs. Erma Sherman Buggage, and there it was, inexplicably alive and well!

I said to Lamart, "Oh my goodness! Look at that plant! Holy crap! It's still alive!"

I gingerly trudged back to the table, unable to believe what I saw. The house hadn't had any lights on for weeks, and no one had been watering those plants. How did this one plant manage to survive? And why was it Miss Erma's plant instead of any of the others?

"Oh my God, can you believe this?" I asked Lamart with a stunned smile. "And look at it! It's not even drooping. It's just sitting there as if I watered it yesterday."

He said in his straightforward tone, "Yeah, that is strange."

The sight of the thriving plant reinforced my sense of wonder. "This is serious. Do you understand what this means? It means that your mom is watching over us, and she's telling us two things: that she is okay, and that we're going to be okay."

Upon saying that, I cradled the plant and carried it to the car. I placed it on the floor of the front passenger seat between my feet, where I carefully guarded it. I brought Erma home to Belle Rose with us.

Erma, our little miracle plant, is still alive, well, and thriving in our current home after twenty years!

# Chapter 9
## It's Waiting for You

To say that my mother-in-law, Erma Buggage, was not exactly doing cartwheels when I entered her son's life is an understatement. Whoo, Lawd, she was tough! Lamart is an only child and was the light of her life. Any woman who has ever married an only child from the deep south knows precisely what I'm talking about! I have known him since I was ten years old, and while he knew my family well, I had never met any of his people. So, in 1997, when I relocated from California to New Orleans to be his girlfriend, let's say the temperature of the reception by my future mother-in-law was a bit colder than the recent snowfall in New Orleans!

My relationship with Miss Erma was amusing. She was a tiny woman, but she carried a big presence. And Lord, could she talk! That lady had the gift of gab like no one I've ever known. Miss Erma could keep a conversation going from sunrise to sunset without taking a breath! Over time, though, I realized that, whether she wanted to admit it or not, I was growing on her. After all, her son was always smiling during our visits; I was always polite (at least in words); and even when she threw a little dig my way, I took it in stride. I truly believe she thought that now, with me around, she would not see her son as much, which was completely wrong. I encouraged him to see her just as often as he always had. In truth,

I was longing for a mother figure of my own. Winning her over became my quiet goal.

She insisted on cooking every Sunday, so every Sunday for the next six years, we went over to Miss Erma's house for dinner. I generally served everyone her delicious food, and I insisted on washing, drying, and putting up the dishes before we left. As the years passed, Miss Erma remained mentally sharp as ever, but her tiny frame was beginning to weaken. On the days when she wasn't up to cooking, I gladly stepped in. I'd prepare full meals in my kitchen, and Lamart and I would bring the food over to her house so we could all share it together. As always, I served the meals and then handled the cleaning of the kitchen afterwards. My mother-in-law really enjoyed my cooking. Miss Erma also loved turkey necks. I often paid a visit to Causey's Restaurant on Chef Highway to pick up a plate of turkey necks on Wednesdays, as this was the specialty of the day. She was delighted to get that meal!

Over time, our love for one another grew, and we did mother/daughter activities. She would let me wash and curl her hair, and she liked playing in my hair. Occasionally, she, or one of her nieces, would polish her nails, but I was the one she chose to remove the polish once it started peeling. She loved to go shopping, especially to Dillard's and Burlington. I would drop her off at the front door and then park so that she would not have to walk far. We would stop to enjoy lunch after having our shopping fill. I also became a little emboldened with her quick and snappy wit, and, in time, I felt comfortable enough to give it back to her.

"Enough, woman!" She would just chuckle because she realized her apprehension about me was misdirected and in a big way. She began referring to me as the daughter she never had, and the first time she said that I cried. *Finally!* I thought.

It was Mother's Day 2004, and I prepared a special dinner for Lamart's parents. Miss Erma loved to cook "Seven Steaks" but hadn't made them in many months. I decided to try making them because I knew how much she, her husband, Jimmy, and my husband enjoyed them. I knew she was disappointed that she could no longer cook like she used to, and, although we offered to take her to a nice restaurant for Mother's Day, she said she'd rather stay home and have me cook something for them. I asked her to tell me how she cooked them, and I followed her instructions. Of course, her recipe had no measurements: a pinch of salt, a sprinkle of onion powder, a whole onion, but not one too big nor too small, about a thimble of pepper, and two or three garlic cloves. That's how cooking is done down here! (The steaks turned out incredibly tasty and tender if you're curious.)

My husband and I also brought her two beautiful Hallmark cards and a small box of sugar-free chocolates that Mother's Day. I always purchased one card from Lamart only, then a second card from both of us. When Miss Erma opened the card from both of us, it featured a beautiful bouquet of magnolias. In her sassiest voice, she snipped, "Vanessa, you gave me this same card last year!"

To which I replied, "Oh, no I didn't!"

"Yes, you did. I remember those flowers."

"Miss Erma, I remember the card I gave you last year. It had red roses all over it. Don't tell me I gave you this card last year!" I sassed.

She was determined, however. "Well, somebody gave me this card last year."

I happened to glance to her left and caught sight of a beautiful white ceramic vase covered in magnolias. I pointed and said, "This is what you're thinking of, Miss Erma. Those flowers on that vase look just like the ones on this card. Maybe that's why I picked it. I know doggone well I didn't get you this same card last year." She looked amazed and said, "Well, I'll be." Her eyes lingered on the vase for a moment, as if seeing it for the first time, and then she gave a small, delighted shake of her head.

*No apology offered, though!*

Sadly, Miss Erma's health worsened in 2004, as if she sensed her time on earth was running out. In later conversations, she asked me if there was anything in the house I wanted to keep.

First, I told her that she wasn't going anywhere! She pressed me, asking if I wanted jewelry, but I told her she could give that to her nieces because I didn't wear much jewelry. However, her sister, Emelda ("Auntie Mel"), had painted ceramic cats for all her sisters—Erma, Annie Mae, Jessie, and Ruth—so each sister had an "Emelda Cat" as well as an "Emelda Rooster" in their homes. I told Miss Erma that, if anything, I would like to have the ceramic cat with the pretty blue eyes that Auntie Mel made for her.

She instructed me to take it right then and there, and I politely refused. She was alive, and I wasn't about to start taking anything from her home. So, she said to Jimmy, her husband, "Vanessa wants the cat." Even with that agreement, I still couldn't bring myself to remove the statue after my mother-in-law's death, because Jimmy was still living in the house. I just couldn't do it.

Miss Erma passed away on January 7, 2005, eight months before the 165 mph winds and flooding waters of Hurricane Katrina destroyed her modest three-bedroom, two-bathroom home of over thirty years. She was a meticulous housekeeper, with a place for everything and everything in its place. With her trinkets and crocheted blankets, Miss Erma created a warm, welcoming, and charming home. While we deeply miss my mother-in-law, we were comforted by the knowledge that she didn't have to witness the damage inflicted on her beloved home.

Miss Erma's house was a raised structure sitting on blocks. What we did not know at the time was that when the house was raised, the contractors did not bolt the foundation to the blocks. As a result, when Katrina's waters surged through the Lower Ninth Ward, Miss Erma's home lurched off its foundation, tilted precariously, and came to rest leaning against the house next door. When Lamart drove up to the house for the first time, he immediately saw a prominent, red notice on the door warning: "Condemned. Do Not Enter!" He didn't exactly follow those directions, but that's our little secret. He walked through the hall of his parents' house to gauge the damage, which was overwhelming. He immediately saw the 32" television he had recently bought, which had floated from the front living area to the kitchen at the back of the house. Their adorable, little kitchen table was upside down, the refrigerator had fallen over, and the etagere in the living room rested face down in the muck.

Several days after the miraculous rescue of my beloved Black Cat, I sat down to carefully examine the photos Lamart had taken of our house and his parents' home. I had been so focused on rescuing Black Cat that I couldn't fully grasp the extent of the damage inflicted on the house where my husband grew up. Sadly, I felt deep in my heart that the chances of saving anything from that house were slim to none. I thought about Miss Erma's gift to me, which I refused when I should have accepted it. In retrospect, would it really have been a bad thing to accept the ceramic kitty while she was still alive? These thoughts only made me feel even sadder. It was then I decided to shift my focus to the cat I did save, my precious, Nubian beauty, Black Cat.

Finally gaining access to New Orleans East, it was time to roll up our sleeves and tackle the enormous cleanup, including cleaning out our house, hauling away debris, and tracking down reliable contractors. Lamart and I made bi-weekly trips to our home, loading our SUV with whatever salvageable items we could fit, and taking them to a storage facility. On the drive from Belle Rose back home, we passed the exit to his mother's house, and each time we did, I felt that Miss Erma wanted me to visit and see if the cat statue had survived the storm.

I mentioned this to my husband each time, and he would say, in no uncertain terms, that there was no way the fragile ceramic cat could have survived the storm and the house tilting without something falling onto the statue and breaking it into a hundred pieces. This went on for several weeks. We would make that bi-weekly trip to New Orleans, I would ask if we could stop by his mom's house, and he would assure me it didn't make sense. He had good reasons. First, the door was ajar when he arrived to take pictures the first time, so whatever was left of any value had probably been taken by looters. Second, the house fell off its foundation and everything rolled over to the left side. From what he could see, the etagere where the cat had perched had fallen forward. He said he felt bad I hadn't taken the cat, but it was too late now.

And yet...every single day, I could sense Miss Erma's voice: "Vanessa, go get your cat!" Every day!

I was left thinking, *Oh, Lord, you can't even keep her quiet in heaven, can you?* It reminded me of Sam Wheat in the movie *Ghost*, following poor Oda Mae Brown all over her house, tormenting her. But Miss Erma wasn't singing *"I'm Henry the 8th, I am."* No, she was yelling, *"I'm telling you to get that cat!"* Same tune, same energy!

Miss Erma penetrated my consciousness and would not give me a break. Her voice was as clear in my ear as when she was alive. At first, I thought it was just me; that I was thinking about the cat, and my conversation with Miss Erma about taking it, and that somehow, I was punishing myself for not accepting the statue when she offered. But then, thinking about the plant she left us from the funeral, the access given when reaching the Morans and the Levys, and finding my precious Black Cat, maybe, just maybe, there really was a chance the statue survived Katrina and was actually waiting for me to go and get it. I had to find out.

I do not remember the exact date I received her final message, but it was probably sometime in mid-October. We were on the interstate transitioning from I-610 to I-10 when Miss Erma gave me my last orders to go to the house and get my cat. As we entered Interstate 10, the first exit was Louisa Drive, which leads to Miss Erma's home. Just before the exit, she snapped at me: "Vanessa, go get your cat!"

I firmly told my husband, "I'm telling you! Your mama is telling me to go and get my cat. Take the exit!"

"Vanessa, are you serious?" He was clearly annoyed. "You can't even get in the house! I don't even go there! You've seen the pictures. There's no way that cat survived. I mean, you probably should have taken it when she offered it to you. Maybe one of the aunts has an extra one (meaning one of Miss Erma's sisters)."

I knew we were in for a battle. He's Leo the Lion and I'm Aries the Ram. He can be strong-willed, and I can be headstrong, so it was a case of letting the games begin!

"Lamart, yes! Yes! I'm telling you. She's in my ear." I began to plead my case. "What's the worst that could happen? I can find the damned thing in a hundred pieces, but at least I'll know.

If I don't go, then I won't know."

He let out a big, aggravated sigh. Clearly, I had struck a nerve, asking one time too many. But this time, I finally got my way. With a quick flick of his index finger, he activated the right turn signal, steered toward the off-ramp, and took the exit. But for the music on the radio, there was no sound. This was our first official tiff since the storm, and we were both holding our ground. He needed to put a stop to this delusion of mine once and for all, and I needed to see if I was truly hearing Miss Erma talk to me or if I was losing my freaking mind.

He grumbled, "You know this is just a waste of time."

I responded with words laced with irritation.

"Well, again, if we don't go, then we won't know! PERIOD!"

*I can be a little snippy, too, Pal! And with yo' mama on my side, it's two against one!*

His parents' house was about two miles from the interstate, so it only took us a few minutes to get there. Dirt and debris were scattered on the local streets, and we had to navigate through a maze of twigs, branches, and logs. Fortunately, my Tahoe sat high, which made it easier for us to maneuver. We kept cleaning supplies and similar items in the SUV in case we needed them, so we were prepared if we found anything salvageable.

Even though I had seen the devastation in pictures, the actual sight of their house took my breath away. Seeing up close my in-law's home off its foundation was heartbreaking. The large red sign on the door: "Condemned. Do Not Enter!" was visible from the car.

I let out another call to the Lord: "Oh, dear God!" This was surreal, but not in a good way. No one in their right mind should enter that house, but here we were, and we had one shot at it. We gingerly climbed the four steps to reach the porch. We could see inside, and once I saw the etagere was flipped forward, for a moment, my heart sank.

My husband, in his favorite yet irritating sarcastic tone, asked, "And just where is Mama telling you that the cat is supposed to be?"

Either I'm psychic or she really said to me, "In the corner to the left." I stated this matter-of-factly.

He said, "Vanessa, the etagere is over there! If it's under there, it's in a million pieces."

"Humor me!" I said.

We came this far, damn it. I am not leaving here until I find it, one way or the other!

As he lifted the etagere, I placed a contractor's bag on the floor to keep my knees away from the smell and toxins of the mud. Thankfully, my hair was in a ponytail, so I didn't have to worry about it touching the filthy ground. Turning my head sideways, I quickly saw what looked like the bottom of the ceramic cat. I exclaimed cautiously, "Oh my God, I see it!"

I reached in about eleven or twelve inches, careful not to let my arm fall into the mud pile that had taken over the once-beautiful hardwood floors of this welcoming home. As I grabbed the statue and slowly pulled it toward me. My heart was racing! In those few seconds, I instinctively knew I would either burst into tears of joy or tears of complete devastation. I would either thank Miss Erma or curse her for playing such a cruel joke on me. I was moments away from discovering what lay ahead.

In those fleeting moments of hesitation, Lamart suddenly broke my trance.

"Come on, girl, this thing's heavy!"

*Grrrrr! Lord, I just wanted to smack him!*

With bated breath, I edged the ceramic cat out from under the etagere, my hands trembling slightly. Every inch it moved felt like a gamble, a delicate dance with fate. I was treading the thin line between joy and sorrow, dreams and reality, surprise and disappointment. I held it up, and there it was, completely intact! Not a single chip, not a crack anywhere. Dirt and grime clung to its surface, and the smell! Oh, the smell! It was worse than anything I'd ever encountered outside of my babies' litter boxes when I returned from being gone for a long weekend! But otherwise, it was flawless. This beautiful, blue-eyed keepsake was yet another little miracle in my hands. I burst into tears and proudly boasted, "I TOLD you your mama wanted me to have this cat!"

Lamart responded in defeat, "Okay, you're good? You got your cat? Let's get outta here."

He already knew he would never live this down. Poor baby. He hated when his mother and I teamed up against him in life, and now she was doing it from heaven.

Then, as if making one final, gentle point, my eyes caught something else. As I carefully carried the ceramic cat toward the front door, I glanced to the right, and there it was: the magnolia vase, the very same one that had inspired the last Mother's Day card we gave Miss Erma before she passed. Sunlight caught its delicate petals just right, and it sat there, completely intact! No chips, no cracks, not a single scratch.

I could not help but smile, tears welling in my eyes, as if she were there, quietly watching and smiling back. "Miss Erma," I whispered, my voice trembling with gratitude, "I guess you wanted me to have that, too. Thank you so much."

I carefully packed them in the cargo area, took them to Belle Rose, washed and sanitized them, and gave them a new home. They have been displayed prominently in our house since 2006.

And for the record, I truly believe Miss Erma's work on this earth is complete. Since I went to gather the gifts she wanted me to have, her voice has fallen silent in my ear. A final confirmation that her work is done. And yet, in that silence, I can still feel the warmth of her presence lingering around me, particularly when I'm watering that beautiful plant that she also left for us.

# Chapter 10

## She Touched Two Sisters

After Katrina, I couldn't reach my sister Vicki or my brother Tony. The hurricane's destruction was so extensive that cell towers were down across many areas, and countless carriers were unable to provide service to their customers.

I knew Vicki, her husband, David, and their son, David Jr. planned to evacuate. Still, with no working cell phone towers, we couldn't reach each other to confirm. Both sides were extremely worried. She knew I was off to Belle Rose, but she had no way of knowing if I left on time or was stranded.

The last call we had was midday on August 26, as I scrambled to prepare the house for the storm. I paused, hands still dusty from packing, and dialed her number.

"Hey, girl, y'all left yet?" I asked, trying to keep my voice light.

"No, but I hope we leave soon. David said traffic is backing up like crazy. What about you? You're going where you usually go, to Belle Rose with Lamart's people, right?"

"Yes," I said. "Monica said we could stay at her house. Lamart's got storm duty, so I won't be seeing him anytime soon. The cats and I are heading out in the next few hours."

"Okay, well, keep me updated on how you make out," she said, worry threading through her tone.

"You do the same, Vicki. I guess we'll see each other in a few days, huh?"

"Hopefully, the storm will turn, but if not… Lord, help us all." Her voice trembled slightly, leaving no doubt that my sister was genuinely frightened by the hurricane bearing down on us.

I was unable to reach my brother to check in, but he left me a voicemail saying he was also preparing to evacuate his residence. He planned to go to our cousin Mitchell's house in Carencro, near Lafayette. I never spoke with Tony on the phone again before the storm to find out his exact location.

As cell phone connectivity slowly became available, Vicki, Tony, and I made calls to our Aunt Ruth, who lived in Corona, California. She became our main connection; each of us called her every few days to check in. This way, if other family members called to report they were safe, she gave us updates. Roughly a week after Katrina, I learned that Tony took refuge at Baptist Hospital in the uptown area of the city. Vicki saw a TV news segment showing Tony on a small boat on Napoleon Avenue, uptown, near the hospital, helping senior citizens onto boats to take them to safety. This news brought me a great sense of relief. Ironically, this is the same hospital where the Morans took shelter during the storm and before being moved to the convention center. Tony did not know the Morans, though.

Communications were restored between Vicki and me first. On the fifth day following the hurricane, she called from a number I did not recognize.

"Hello?"

"Hey, girl! Lawd, thank goodness! Ya'll all right?" She was almost breathless with her inquiry.

"Girl, hey!" I responded with massive relief. "Where are you guys?"

"We're in Lake Charles, Louisiana."

Puzzled, I asked, "Lake Charles? Dang! How did y'all wind up all the way up there?"

"We just kept driving and driving, looking for a vacant hotel. Finally, we ended up at this church in Lake Charles, and that's where we are now. At first, we were inside the church, but now we have an apartment."

With genuine relief, I said, "Oh my goodness, Vicki! Well, at least y'all are safe."

We resumed talking as if no time had passed since our last daily conversation. Vicki explained that the people there were very kind and went out of their way to help those who had evacuated from New Orleans. Despite their kindness, my sister was worried, like many others, about whether her home would still be there when she returned. Then, she shared a rather unusual story. That wispy quality colored her voice.

"Vanessa, the strangest thing happened. I met this lady. She was so sweet. Honestly, I think she was an angel. We stayed in the church our first couple of nights here, with all those people. Even though they were all very nice, we felt very uncomfortable. You know me, I'm a homebody, and I couldn't help wondering how bad the damage in our house was going to be. But this lady, somehow, ended up near us, and we started talking. Then, she asked me if I wanted to pray with her, and it was just what the doctor ordered. It made me feel so much better. She was very comforting."

She continued, "This woman took my hands into hers and began saying the Our Father, and we prayed that prayer together. Then, she started praying with her own words. My eyes were closed as she prayed, and her voice was angelic. She asked the Lord to keep my family safe and bring us peace. When she finished, I felt really calm. I truly did."

"She does sound like an angel, Vicki."

"And the strangest thing is that she knew all about our family, the Despenzas. She actually claimed to have ancestors with our last name."

I was in shock. "Are you serious?"

"Yeah! She knew about our grandfather; she knew about his nightclub, the Shadowland, and its history; that it was listed in the Green Book, and that it lasted over forty years, I mean, everything. She knew our grandfather was a musician, and how prominent the family name was in the music and entertainment industry. I mean, she knew a lot!"

I responded cautiously but kept an open mind. She really could be an angel. What are the chances that my sister would meet someone in Lake Charles, a city about three hundred miles away, who knew the Despenza name and its legacy?

"That IS strange." My curious mind now wanted to know: "What did she look like? Did y'all exchange phone numbers?"

"That's the strange thing, Vanessa. It was like she was there that night, and by the next morning, she was gone. That's why I'm saying, I think she was an angel."

"Well, she might very well have been, Vicki. You know, if anyone is going to believe you, it's me!"

Vicki, self-questioning, responded, "I didn't think to get a phone number from her. I just remember she said she lives on the West Bank."

Vicki and I were both living on the East Bank (New Orleans) at the time of the storm. Because the city has so many amenities, we rarely found ourselves visiting the West Bank; that's the area located across the Mississippi River from New Orleans. We usually refer to each area as the East Bank or the West Bank. My only recent visit to the West Bank was when Angie and I traveled to the Algiers Naval Base to rescue the Morans. Vicki did not get the name of the West Bank city where the lady lived (if, in fact, she isn't an angel). I knew we had some cousins over on the West Bank. I never met them, but maybe she's one of those Despenzas. *Interesting*, I thought.

Vicki truly couldn't remember this lady's name, only that she was very pretty with long, dark hair. She told me she had planned to find out the woman's name as soon as she saw her again, but when she woke up the next morning, the lady was gone.

It was a positive yet uncanny encounter. What were the odds that, all the way in Lake Charles, a three-hour drive from New Orleans, at that very church, with hundreds of people, Vicki would run into a distant relative? Someone who knew so much about our family and then disappeared as mysteriously as she had appeared?

Perhaps the explanation lay in geography: the woman lived on one side of the Mississippi River while we lived on the other, and the two sides of the family may never have crossed paths in our generation. And yet, out of more than two hundred people in the church, how did this woman come to approach, pray with, and comfort Vicki and her family, rather than anyone else? It felt like something greater had guided her steps, a quiet nudge of destiny, placing the right person in the right place at exactly the right moment.

In any case, life went on, and the process of healing, rebuilding, and reconstructing began. Lamart and I moved to a smaller city on the northern side of Lake Pontchartrain in 2006. Vicki still lives in her New Orleans home, which was thankfully spared. While life after Katrina is different than before her arrival, we have all managed to survive and move forward.

Fast forward to 2022 – I retired from my role as a Human Resources professional and decided to focus on my health. Covid took a toll on me since I was working extremely long hours remotely, which meant a lot of sitting. Additionally, after losing my brother and my beloved nephew, along with six in-laws, I gained weight and exercised much less. To counter this, I joined a program where I worked with a "coach" who provided nutritional advice to support her clients' fitness journeys. I stayed in the program for over a year and managed to lose about twenty pounds.

Around that time, I began thinking seriously about writing this book. Nearly twenty years had passed since Katrina, and I felt an urgency to preserve these experiences on paper before the details faded with time. One chapter I knew I wanted to include was about Vicki's angel. I called my sister to pick her brain, asking what she remembered about the woman who had comforted her during such a dark and frightening time. I pressed for details; such as the name of the church, and any other pieces she could recall that might bring the encounter back into focus.

Wistfully, she offered, "Oh, Vanessa, all I can tell you is that she was very pretty, and she had long, dark hair and a nice smile." But this time she mentioned something that I did not recall hearing. "All I know is that she had a gym on the West Bank. I don't know the name of it."

Interestingly, my coach in this nutrition program had a gym on the West Bank during Katrina. During a training session with her, I found out we shared the same great-grandfather. However, I never considered that my former coach could be the person Vicki met all those years ago, and that she came back into our lives as my nutrition coach. Now the hairs on the back of my neck stood up. "Vicki, I think I know who your angel is!" I said.

I immediately messaged the woman in question, my heart pounding as I typed: *"Where did you evacuate for Katrina? By chance, were you in Lake Charles?"*

A few minutes later, her reply popped up: *"Yes. We were in Lake Charles at a church for a couple of nights, and then we left early to head to Texas."*

My breath caught. I pressed on: *"Do you remember praying with a lady who was a Despenza?"*

Her answer came back quickly: *"Yes. I remember talking with a lady, her son, and her husband. And yes, we prayed together."*

That was it. My fingers flew across the keyboard: *"Oh my God! That lady is my sister, Vicki!"*

Her response came in a rush: *"Are you serious??!!!!"*—exclamation marks spilling across the screen.

*"Yes!"* I shot back, my hands trembling now.

I kept typing, tears welling up as I wrote: *"Do you realize this has been a mystery for the past nineteen years? And now we finally have our answer!"*

I sat back, stunned. After all these years, the question that had lingered like a whisper was finally answered. And yet, given everything that had happened in those chaotic days and weeks after Katrina, part of me wasn't surprised at all. By now, I could believe just about anything.

So, although she may not have appeared with white-feathered wings or a glowing halo, I believe that on that night, for my sister and her family, this distant cousin was heaven-sent. An earthly angel, placed in their path to bring comfort, reassurance, and a reminder that even in the darkest storm, God's light can still break through.

# Chapter 11

## One Last Miracle

My goal has always been to work in a profession where I could write, whether as a novelist, journalist, technical writer, or screenwriter. As a child, I filled pages with poems and stories about my dolls, friends, pets, and family. I would give anything to hold those little treasures in my hands still today.

Unfortunately, I didn't get much support at home to pursue writing as a career. Instead, life took me down a different, unexpected path; one that led me through roles like an executive assistant, an Artist Relations liaison at independent record labels, an office manager at a drug treatment center for parenting moms, a legal secretary, a paralegal, and later, an HR professional.

Yet in every single job, I always found a way to write. Jingles, party and event invitations, biographies, album reviews, and company newsletters. You name it, I wrote it. Writing was the thread that ran quietly but persistently through everything I did.

But I never wrote a book. Not until now. It's taken me a long time to finally arrive here, holding my first manuscript, the dream I've carried with me all along.

When I retired from Human Resources in 2022, I was ready to start my writing career. However, I wanted some time for myself to redecorate, create a sewing room in my house, travel, and relax before I began researching and setting aside quiet time to start this book. Two months into this break, a former coworker contacted me and referred me to her new employer to set up their entire HR system. What began as a two-month gig quickly expanded, and I was soon approached by other former colleagues for additional HR specialized projects. Although I enjoyed the independent opportunities, time was running out. Over two years passed before I realized it, and I hadn't even written a Table of Contents.

So, now it's spring 2024, and I'm working long hours for my three clients. I still haven't had time for my book. I knew since I hadn't written creatively in many years, it would take some time to find my artistic rhythm, and I really needed the help of a writing coach and an editor.

To my dismay, when I started researching the costs of writing and self-publishing a book, I realized I was unprepared for this effort. The average cost to self-publish a book, including marketing, promotion, printing, website development, artwork, copyrighting, and other expenses, can reach upwards of $15,000 or more. Launching a book is much more than writing the story, sending the manuscript to the printer, and hoping the book sells on its own. I knew from years in the music business that when a CD is released, it requires marketing, promotion, networking, and other efforts; and those costs add up! I wanted to give my book the best chance for success, and cutting corners was not an option. With that reality in mind, I knew I had to move forward carefully and systematically.

I had to consider my next step. Should I go back to work for a couple of years to save up my writer's nest egg? Since retiring, I've been approached by several companies that were familiar with me through my former coworkers for full-time roles. But the truth was that I loved my last and final full-time job. I spent over fourteen years there, and that was the place I planned to retire from; there wasn't going to be any other company after that. The idea of retiring from anywhere else wasn't an option.

So, here I was, facing this dilemma. How would I fund this book? Doubts began to creep in. That little voice inside launched into a full-blown argument: "Maybe it is NOT time for you to write this book. We have an upcoming election, and regardless of who wins, might some changes impact your life and/or your retirement income? What about taxes? Might it be necessary for you to work full-time for a few more years?" I was in a strange emotional place. I was still taking on small, short-term HR projects here and there because I enjoyed the work, but I felt deep down that I really wanted to write, not tie myself down to a full-time job. I was caught in a catch-22. I needed money to invest in myself.

It was Memorial Day in 2024. Family was coming over, and I was cooking up a storm. Hamburgers, pork ribs, baked beans, red beans (yes, two types of beans), potato salad, coleslaw, hot dogs, fried chicken, and a large assortment of cookies from Sam's Club. The topic of my book came up, and family members questioned the status. I didn't have an answer. I only said I planned to have it finished by the twentieth anniversary of Katrina, which was a little over a year away. I don't know if I was lying to them or to myself, or if I was caught up in a blaze of wishful thinking.

Later that evening, after everyone had left and my husband was asleep in his recliner, the house was tranquil, and I kept thinking about the conversation with the family and their questions about my book's progress. After all, I had been talking about this book for years, and they had been encouraging me to share my stories for just as long. I knew several things. When it came to creative writing, I was rusty. I remembered from my work with independent record labels that most first releases did not sell millions of copies, and that professionals were best suited to handle marketing and promotion. I also knew I was too practical to dip into my retirement savings and spend that kind of money on a gamble like a book from a wannabe writer who hadn't written creatively in years. Also, someone who lacked the resources to produce, market, and promote the book herself. So, what was I supposed to do? I needed guidance from a higher power.

I took the serenity of the moment as the perfect chance to pray to God, asking for guidance. To avoid waking my hubby or the fur babies, I quietly tiptoed to the side of my bed and knelt. I explained to God that I really, REALLY, wanted to finish my book in time for Katrina's twentieth anniversary. Because of the many tragedies the country, and even the world, had seen in the two decades since Katrina, I wanted my little book to serve as a beacon of hope; something that, if a person felt alone, they could turn to and think, "If Vanessa was able to find peace by opening her heart to the possibility of her little miracles, maybe there are some little miracles out there for me. And if I keep an open mind, maybe that will help me discover them."

When I prayed, I didn't ask for money to fund the book. That would be sacrilegious. I asked the Lord to give me the direction I needed. Was the book meant to be written at this time? Maybe a year from now, or perhaps for the twenty-fifth anniversary of Katrina? I needed clarity. So, I prayed.

*Dear God, yes, I know. I'm on a bended knee. You're not used to seeing me pray like this, on these lovely knees that You gave me that I have abused over the years. But this is super important, Lord. I need guidance, and since you're my guiding light, I'm asking you to shine it just a little brighter so I can see where I am supposed to be headed.*

*I'm eager to quit my little day jobs and focus on writing my book. Despite planning for retirement, and you KNOW I did, three years later, it's tough out here. I pay my bills, and my credit is excellent, but I don't have $15,000 or more in unrestricted funds to finance this book. Are you telling me I should go back to work for a few years, save some money, and write later? That now isn't the right time? Show me the way, and I'll gladly follow it, no matter where it leads. I've set aside my retirement funds for rainy days, not for my creative whims. But if that's the message I'm receiving from you, I'll do it. You've given me the ability to tell a good story. People have said that to me for decades. And of all my stories, and Lord, you know better than anyone that I have plenty, this is the one I really want to tell. So, what am I supposed to do? I'm all ears! Amen!*

Deep down, I believed returning to work was the answer. I was so sure that I opened my laptop that evening and updated my resume. I had expected the phone to ring, and someone would offer me another full-time opportunity. No matter what it was, I was ready to accept. However, I never received a call from a potential employer.

Three weeks after I invoked that prayer, I received an unexpected text message. It was an invitation to lunch from an executive at a company where, during its startup phase, I had once worked closely with him. I had not spoken with him in many years, though we occasionally texted. Even after leaving the company, I remained on his family's Christmas card list, and I always looked forward to their custom cards, which were the perfect mix of funny and endearing. The cards also let me see how their children grew into adulthood.

Receiving the text at this moment was a surprise, though a pleasant one. I had been following the company on social media, so I knew Brian's business had recently expanded and was doing remarkably well. The message was a friendly invitation to meet Brian and his wife, Karen, for a meal at 11:30 a.m. at a rather upscale restaurant, which was no surprise, given Brian's penchant for doing things in style.

The day we were scheduled to meet was a wet one! The weather forecast called for rain throughout the day. The restaurant's parking lot was not especially large, so I knew I would have to park on the street. Luckily, or God's will, someone was pulling away from a spot very close to the restaurant just as I arrived in search of a space. Yay!

Karen and I arrived at the same time. She wore her usual bright smile, and we greeted each other with a big hug. We talked about our families, and within a few minutes, Brian arrived. We once again discussed family, and the conversation quickly shifted to their company. I mentioned that I had been following their growth on LinkedIn and had heard about their recent expansion. I expressed my pride in having worked there and my admiration for what Brian had achieved.

He spoke with ease, recounting the history of what had unfolded since I left the company, detailing corporate decisions, milestones, and the choices that had shaped the business. I listened intently, fascinated not only by what he shared but also by the privilege of glimpsing the story from the inside.

Then, as our plates sat nearly empty, Brian set his fork down with quiet finality. He reached for his glass, took a slow sip of water, and paused. The table was silent. And then, leaning in slightly, he began to unravel the mystery behind this invitation, a revelation that would lead to the very last little miracle in this book.

"Well, I'm sure you're wondering why we wanted to have lunch with you."

Brian always kept more on the "matter of fact" side, so at this point, I had no idea what he was going to say next.

And then he uttered seven simple one-syllable words.

"We want to give you a gift."

My head spun. *A gift? Oh my goodness! Really?*

"This is our way of showing just how much we appreciate you and everything you did to help us in the early months of our business venture. You gave so much of yourself, working hard and standing by us with fierce loyalty, always looking out for my partners and me. You weren't just part of the process; you were a vital part of the company's success. Karen and I have talked about it, and we both feel strongly that we want to give you something meaningful."

I expected a small box, perhaps holding a lovely necklace, a gift card, a scarf, or a souvenir from one of their trips abroad. I was NOT prepared for what he said next.

Still, in his uniquely kind yet professional style, he looked me directly in the eyes and said, "We would like to give you a monetary gift."

I sat upright, still, motionless.

And then he revealed the amount.

*Wait! What?*

My brain whirled and processed.

*I think he said this amount, but I could be wrong. Surely, with the heavy raindrops tapping on the restaurant window, I might have misunderstood. He couldn't have said that. There's no way!*

I sat quietly, examining and reasoning, as I do so well. I didn't want to mess this up by assuming something that wasn't there. There was apparent stillness and silence at the table as I tried to gather my thoughts.

*But then*, I thought, *during all the years I have known and worked with this gentleman, I've never once misunderstood anything he's ever said.*

I felt my eyes tear up, but I was determined to stay composed. I looked at Brian, then I looked at Karen. She was smiling.

I considered asking, *"Brian, Karen, are you guys serious? I mean, I know you are. You would never joke about something like this."* But instead, I ask the dumbest question in the world: "Are you sure?"

Of course they were. This man is one of the most methodical people I have ever known.

Brian continued, "Yes, and we can give this amount as a tax-free gift, so you will not have to pay any taxes on it. It's our way of saying thank you."

I looked at Karen again, and it was as if she knew what I was about to ask.

"Yes, we both want you to have this. Although I may not have worked there, I've always been aware of your dedication. I could not be more supportive of this."

*Holey Freaking Moley!*

*No. <u>HOLY</u> Moley!*

As surprising as the gift was, who it was from was really no surprise.

Growing up with my grandmother, by the time she had raised her five children and then my sister, my brother, and me, there wasn't much money to send me to college. So, I went straight to work, but I always wanted to earn my degree.

By the time I went to work at Brian's company, I had earned approximately sixty credits toward my degree. I used to tell people I graduated with honors from OJT University because I felt I had learned the real world on the job. Still, I wanted that formal education more than anything.

About a year after I started working at Brian's company, the owners agreed to introduce a tuition reimbursement benefit, and I took advantage of it. With the tuition reimbursement offered by Brian's company, I was able to earn my degree with honors, and three years later, I went on to earn my MBA with honors as well.

The graduation ceremony for my bachelor's was in Baton Rouge. I hadn't sent invitations to anyone, expecting only my husband to be there as my cheerleader. After the ceremony, I moved through the crowd to find Lamart, and who else was there but Brian! Now, keep in mind, I saw him in the office the day before, and he never acknowledged my graduation all day. I knew he was aware of it. As we were the last two to leave the building that day, I said good night to him. His back was turned, so he gestured and said "Good night," and that was it.

Admittedly, I was a little disappointed that he didn't wish me well as I left, but I thought, *"He's really into whatever it is he's working on,"* and let it go. I guessed he didn't know what was going on, but, boy, was I wrong. He had a partner in crime in the office, Anne, who asked me earlier in the day about the location and time of the ceremony. He had told her to find out all the details because he had planned to be there all along.

When I saw him in the auditorium, I was moved. I knew he and Karen had family visiting that weekend. He had mentioned that earlier in the week. Yet, he left his house, family, and guests, and drove the seventy miles to the event center to wish me well and congratulate me.

When I saw him, I exclaimed in shock, "Oh my goodness! What are YOU doing here?"

He responded, smiling, "Where else would I be? This is your big day!"

He told me he was determined to come and congratulate me. I was so heartened. I couldn't believe that Brian had driven all that way just for me.

So, can you see how easy it is to recognize that, although the gift was a miracle in response to a prayer for guidance, the person God inspired to create this unexpected little miracle for me was the best possible choice?

That day at the restaurant, when they shared their gift with me, Brian told me that he and Karen both live by the adage that "It's a blessing to be a blessing." They have always been a family rooted in faith, generosity, and charity. When I heard that quote, it resonated with me so profoundly that I had to include it in this chapter. It is deeply inspiring and something worth striving for.

Right then, I knew God had answered my prayers. I couldn't contain my excitement and blurted out, "Guys, you are not going to believe this, but literally, three weeks before you sent me the invitation for lunch, I was on my knees praying to God. I was more than ready to write and self-publish my book. I had planned meticulously, paid off my bills before retirement, and set everything in order, but dreams do have a cost. While I had enough to live on, I didn't have the funds to actually bring my dream to life. And with this gift, now I do!"

I told them that I knew exactly what I would do with that money; I was going to invest in myself and my book, and that they were the "angel investors" that God sent to me. I think it was a bit much for them to take in at first, but when they saw the glow on my face, I could tell they realized they had done something not just special but extraordinary.

As I drove home through the relentless downpour, raindrops streaking the windshield like tiny prisms, my mind wandered back to Hurricane Katrina and the string of little miracles that had brightened those dark days. Could this lunch with Brian and Karen be another thread in that same tapestry of grace? In my heart, it felt undeniably so. And though it didn't occur in 2005, this heavenly intervention is the reason why you are reading this book today; a testament to timing, faith, prayer, and the unseen hands that guide us through our journey on this earth.

What inspired Brian and Karen to think of me after all these years and offer such a generous gift? I can't say. Why now? Why at this precise moment, just weeks after I had prayed to God, seeking guidance on whether it was the right time to move forward with my manuscript?

All I know is that my heart overflows with gratitude. Brian and Karen would rather not receive recognition, yet I want them to know that their kindness and generosity opened this door for me. I will carry that gratitude with me forever.

And if this little book of mine finds its way into the world, I hope to pay that grace forward to someone who was kind to me in the past. Perhaps, in that moment, my gift to them will become their little miracle; arriving exactly when needed, just as mine did!

# Chapter 12

## The Why for This Book

I have recounted these stories with family and friends over the years, and most, if not all, have strongly encouraged me to author a book and share my experiences with a broader audience. It has taken me almost twenty years to put pen to paper, which made me ask myself, "Why now?"

Well, I can say I wanted the book to be released in time for the twentieth anniversary of Katrina, hoping it might bring comfort to wounds that might be reopened or some that may never have healed. But this led me to question, "Why should I even be concerned about when the book is written?" Many people have motivated me and given me the courage to write about these experiences on paper. I realized that it was imperative to share my stories now, given the stark contrast between the overwhelming sadness and happiness in the world. Life truly turns on a dime. As we navigated closer to the twentieth anniversary of the storm, I had a change of heart. I decided that I would release it "when the time was right," and whether that was before the anniversary date or after, remained to be seen. As it turns out, that inner voice, you know the one I'm talking about, determined that it would be better to wait. The stories of Katrina had to be told before the anniversary and on the anniversary date, because they were everyone's stories. The stories shared in this book belong to only a handful of people. This book needed to come later.

What I love about sharing my little miracles is discovering how many others in my circle have also shared theirs with me. Yes, some of their wonders happened right after the storms, just like mine, but others have occurred in the years since. Listening to others' stories only strengthens my belief that what I experienced after Katrina was truly miraculous. I wasn't the only one involved in these blessings. There were the Morans; the Levys; my ex-boss and his wife; my husband, Lamart; my sister, Vicki; my heavenly mother-in-law, Miss Erma; our distant cousin; my beloved Black Cat; and even inanimate keepsakes like Miss Erma's plant, vase, and ceramic kitty.

I learned three truths from my little miracle experiences about life on this earth: 1) You must be open to the idea that forces exist beyond our perception, 2) You should accept that not everything that happens to us is within our control, and 3) Never lose hope. Tomorrow is another day.

Let's face it; it's all too easy to dismiss these ideas. For example, most people can accept that bad things happen to us that are painful and not our fault. And, yes, for those of faith, many are quick to question God and ask, "Why?" Lord knows I've done this more than a few times. Believers accept that certain events in their lives are the will of God. Yet, when positive things happen unexpectedly, we often take them at face value too, without considering how we received the blessing on an ordinary day. Why don't we say these positive, unforeseen events are also God's will? Personally, I believe these much-needed positive occurrences are gifts from heaven and God Almighty. Several times, I've encountered situations that seem unexplainable by ordinary means, including two instances where my life was spared. These events happened many years ago, but I felt a clear intervention from heaven to save me, sensing my grandmother's presence.

On January 21, 2025, the city of New Orleans received ten inches of snow, the most recorded since 1895. Indeed, this was an act of nature, and no one would call it a miracle, but wouldn't it be nice if you could? What if you could take everyday life and focus on just one unique and unexpected event that directly affects you in a positive and uplifting way? What if, for a moment, you consider it a gift or miracle from God, the angels, or a deceased family member you still talk to when no one else is around? If you are not of faith, perhaps it was a gift of karma, the stars, or some other phenomenon. How special would that make you feel? And if not special, then at least blessed.

I believe, whether you have faith in God or not, there are times when you ask yourself, "How did that even happen?" Whether it was a miracle from heaven, the stars aligning just right, a good deed being returned with positive energy, or a wish sent out into the universe being heard, some manifestations on this earth cannot be explained. Yet, that doesn't stop us from experiencing the greatest joy from them.

The moments in this book are my little miracles. Stay receptive to those little miracles you might experience. I genuinely believe there are more coming — not just for me, but for you as well.

Be blessed!

# Bibliography

*10 Years after Hurricane Katrina: The Sea Service Response - USNI News.* (2015, August 31). USNI News. https://news.usni.org/2015/08/31/10-years-after-hurricane-katrina-the-sea-service-response (site no longer accessible)

"14 days - A timeline | The Storm | FRONTLINE | PBS." 2015. November 18, 2015. https://www.pbs.org/wgbh/pages/frontline/storm/etc/cron.html.

Bytheway, Bill. 2024. "The Evacuation of Older People: The Case of Hurricane Katrina." *Items* (blog). February 1, 2024. https://items.ssrc.org/understanding-katrina/the-evacuation-of-older-people-the-case-of-hurricane-katrina/.

Burnett, John. 2015. "At a shelter of last resort, decency prevailed over depravity." *NPR*, August 25, 2015. https://www.npr.org/2015/08/25/431909047/at-a-shelter-of-last-resort-decency-prevailed-over-depravity.

*CNN Coverage of Mayor Nagin, August 28, 2005 - Search Videos.* (n.d.). https://www.bing.com/videos/riverview/relatedvideo?pglt=299&q=cnn+coverage+of+mayor+nagin+august+28%2c+2005&cvid=d1148f98b73f4a98b928594e357cdcb4&gs_lcrp=EgRlZGdlKgYIABBFGDkyBggAEEUYOTIGCAEQABhAMgYIAhBFGDsyBggDEAAYQDIGCAQQABhAMgYIBRAAGEAyBggGEAAYQDIGCAcQRRg8MgYICBBFGDzSAQkxNDEyOGowajGoAgiwAgE&PC=DCTS&ru=%2fsearch%3fpglt%3d299%26q%3dc

nn%2bcoverage%2bof%2bmayor%2bnagin%2baugust%2b28%2
52C%2b2005%26cvid%3dd1148f98b73f4a98b928594e357cdcb4
%26gs_lcrp%3dEgRlZGdlKgYIABBFGDkyBggAEEUYOTIG
CAEQABhAMgYIAhBFGDsyBggDEAAYQDIGCAQQABhA
MgYIBRAAGEAyBggGEAAYQDIGCAcQRRg8MgYICBBFG
DzSAQkxNDEyOGowajGoAgiwAgE%26FORM%3dANNTA1
%26PC%3dDCTS&mmscn=vwrc&mid=76E1B8D00AC7D46A
D89E76E1B8D00AC7D46AD89E&FORM=WRVORC&ntb=1
&msockid=003c6a48677811f0b2e9755a9f961df6.

Drye, Willie. "Hurricane Katrina: The essential timeline." *Science*.
https://www.nationalgeographic.com/science/article/weather-hurricane-katrina-timeline

Fraga. n.d. "Why The Miracle On The Hudson Was Truly As Miraculous As It Seemed."
https://allthatsinteresting.com/miracle-on-the-hudson

Getlen, Larry. 2014. "The Untold Story of How the Buried Chilean Miners Survived." *New York Post*, October 12, 2014. https://nypost.com/2014/10/11/how-the-chilean-miners-men-survived-for-69-days-beneath-the-earths-surface/.

Haygood, Will and Tyson, Ann Scott. *Convention center left legacy of chaos, violence*. (2005, September 15). NBC News. https://www.nbcnews.com/id/wbna9345608

Employment Security Commission. 2024. "NCESC - Discovering Employment Paths and Travel Experiences." Discovering Employment Paths and Travel Experiences. March

20, 2024. https://www.ncesc.com/geographic-faq/how-much-money-did-hurricane-katrina-cost.

Ho, Charlize. 2024. "Hurricane Katrina." *ArcGIS StoryMaps*, December 2, 2024. https://storymaps.arcgis.com/stories/efb679c3955240ab9cb00025d4ef7435.

*Hurricane Katrina - Gulf Islands National Seashore.* (2025, February 13). U.S. National Park Service. https://www.nps.gov/guis/learn/historyculture/hurricane-katrina.htm.

*Hurricane Katrina - Facts, Affected Areas & Lives Lost.* (2025, August 13). History.com Editors. https://www.history.com/articles/hurricane-katrina

McNamara, Dave. "New Orleans Snow Day." *The Heart of Louisiana*, January 22, 2025. https://heartoflouisiana.com/new-orleans-snow/.

Miracle. (2025). In *Merriam-Webster Dictionary*. https://www.merriam-webster.com/dictionary/miracle

Plyer, Allison. 2025. "Facts for Features: Katrina Impact | the Data Center." May 6, 2025. https://www.datacenterresearch.org/data-resources/katrina/facts-for-impact/.

Pruitt, Sarah. 2025. "Hurricane Katrina: 10 facts about the deadly storm and its legacy | HISTORY." HISTORY. June 30, 2025. https://www.history.com/articles/hurricane-katrina-facts-legacy.

Rushton, Christine. 2015. "Timeline: Hurricane Katrina and the aftermath." *USA TODAY*, August 28, 2015. https://www.usatoday.com/story/news/nation/2015/08/24/timeline-hurricane-katrina-and-aftermath/32003013/.

Smith, Patrick. *New Details on Amazon Jungle Plane Crash and Children Who Survived.* (2023, June 13.) NBC News. https://www.nbcnews.com/news/world/how-4-children-survived-40-days-jungle-plane-crash-amazon-colombia-rcna88791.

Sullivan, Laura. 2005. "How New Orleans' evacuation plan fell apart." *NPR*, September 23, 2005. https://www.npr.org/2005/09/23/4860776/how-new-orleans-evacuation-plan-fell-apart.

The Editors of Encyclopaedia Britannica. 2025. "Hurricane Katrina | Deaths, damage, & Facts." Encyclopedia Britannica. August 16, 2025. https://www.britannica.com/event/Hurricane-Katrina.

*What Hurricanes Have Hit Louisiana in Recorded History? How Strong Were They? Here's a List | Hurricane Center | nola.com – Bing.* (n.d.), https://www.bing.com/search?pglt=299&q=What+hurricanes+have+hit+Louisiana+in+recorded+history%3F+How+strong+were+they%3F+Here%27s+a+list+%7C+Hurricane+Center+%7C+nola.com&cvid=056f9b1246294cd2bfa9a04b53eed901&gs_lcrp=EgRIZGdlKgYIABBFGDsyBggAEEUYOzIGCAEQRRg80gEJMTIwMDdqMGoxqAIIsAIB&FORM=ANNTA1&PC=DCTS.

*What Kind of Damage Did Katrina Do in the Bahamas - Bing.* (n.d.). Microsoft Bing CoPilot.

https://www.bing.com/search?pglt=299&q=what+kind+of+damage+did+katrina+do+in+the+bahamas&cvid=c7edb92683ef46858383978b289e7c49&gs_lcrp=EgRlZGdlKgYIABBFGDkyBggAEEUYOdIBCDcyODBqMGoxqAIIsAIB&FORM=ANNTA1&PC=U531&dayref=1

*What Was the Process of Leaving New Orleans before Katrina - Bing.* (n.d.). Microsoft Bing CoPilot.

https://www.bing.com/search?pglt=299&q=what+was+the+process+of+leaving+new+orleans+before+katrina&cvid=cea82e3aa4be4259a265dc7809e0

Weather Channel. 2019. "Cone of Uncertainty: Facts and Myths About This Tropical Forecasting Tool." *The Weather Channel Editors*, May 1, 2019.

https://weather.com/science/weather-explainers/news/tropical-storm-cyclone-forecast-cone-hurricane.

*When Did Katrina Hit Florida - Bing.* (n.d.). Microsoft Bing CoPilot.

https://www.bing.com/search?pglt=299&q=when+did+katrina+hit+florida&cvid=478351f314414c059c71a3ed4e7f3afa&gs_lcrp=EgRlZGdlKgYIABBFGDkyBggAEEUYOTIGCAEQABhAMgYIAhAAGEAyBggDEAAYQDIGCAQQABhAMgYIBRAAGEAyBggGEAAYQDIGCAcQABhAMgYICBAAGEDSAQg2ODIzajBqMagCCLACAQ&FORM=ANNTA1&PC=U531&dayref=1

## Acknowledgements

There have been so many people who have consistently encouraged me to sit down and tell my stories. First and foremost, I give glory to God Almighty for giving me some level of talent to create and to write.

My sister, Vicki, is, and has always been, my rock. I don't know of any two sisters who are closer than Vicki and me. We tell each other everything. She was so encouraging in this process, advising me to "think big" and not underestimate the power of my words. Thank you, Sis. I love you more than there are words to say!

My heart and my thanks to my husband, Lamart, for his awesome sense of humor and for keeping me laughing on a regular basis. His encouragement and his providing me the quiet time to write is sincerely appreciated.

Thank you, Dr. Lana Joseph, for all of your amazing assistance in getting me set up in social media and giving me the benefit of your marketing expertise. Your help has been invaluable!

Kudos to my bestie, Sheryl Boudy, who is a published author herself. She gave me so much of her time and energy, showing me the ropes about the process of writing a book, self-publishing, creating a buzz, and so much more.

Thank you to my friend, Lisa Leonardi, who was so encouraging in this process, and who provided me with amazing marketing tips. She is a Facebook and Instagram influencer, and has introduced me to her massive fan base, encouraging them to purchase my book. Sending love to Bubbacini, Polly, and Rosie.

I would like to acknowledge my writing coach and editor, Michelle Schacht, who turned my ordinary words into magic. She taught me so much in these recent months, and I do not believe this book could have been crafted the way I had hoped for without her. She is amazing, and I look forward to working with her on my next book!

Thank you, Lynn Ashley, Milton Kirby, Janice Wilson, and Rosemary W. for taking the time to conduct a Peer Review and provide me with your candid thoughts and great suggestions to improve my book.

Thank you, Monica Moran, for your hospitality, and for filling in some missing pieces to the story of the Morans.

Finally, my sincerest gratitude to Brian and Karen, who so generously recognized my loyalty and devotion to their business venture, and who blessed me with the means to create and market this book. I will be forever grateful, and I commit to paying it forward should the opportunity arise.

# About the Author

M.V. Despenza was born and raised in New Orleans, LA, as the youngest of three siblings. When her mom died in 1957, she was just under two years old. She, along with her five-year-old brother Tony and her older sister Vicki, who was seven, was raised by their paternal grandmother, Maggie Boudreaux Despenza.

She attended three different elementary schools: Mary D. Coghill, Holy Ghost Catholic School, and St. Gabriel the Archangel. She earned her high school diploma from St. Joseph's Academy, attended several universities, ultimately earning both her bachelor's and master's degrees from the University of Phoenix. She also holds two Human Resources certifications from the Society for Human Resource Management (SHRM) and the Human Resources Certification Institute (HRCI), as well as two credentials from SHRM for Inclusive Workplace and People Analytics. She still gets together regularly with her grammar school friends from Holy Ghost. She treasures those lifelong friendships.

Vanessa grew up in the historic neighborhood of Pontchartrain Park, a community she still holds very close to her heart. She remains deeply connected to many of the friends she grew up with there and shares a special bond that only exists among those who grew up in "The Park."

Vanessa is deeply spiritual and believes that relatives who have passed away still watch over us, and sometimes, they will make their presence known when needed.

When she is not writing, she loves to go on bike rides and nature walks. She considers herself a bit of a hippie, often marveling at a beautiful sunset. She enjoys music and listens to her favorite oldies every day. She loves Luther Vandross! Enjoying and relaxing through other people's creativity and artistry is a key part of staying relaxed and getting into the right mindset to pursue her own creativity. She hopes that now, with this book finished, she can return to another of her favorite hobbies, which involves using her sewing, embroidery, and serger machines.

Vanessa is married to Lamart Buggage and is the proud mama of three cats: two females, Simba and Stella Bella, and one male, Vanilla Bean. However, she will feed any and every animal that comes to her door, whether they are dogs, cats, birds, ducks, squirrels, possums, raccoons, or rabbits. She loves country life, enjoying nature and its many creatures. She enjoys laughing and has a quirky sense of humor.

She enjoys laughter and has a quirky sense of humor. Though extremely camera-shy, she understands that for her stories to be shared, she must occasionally step beyond her comfort zone so her experiences can inspire and touch others.

[1] Plyer, Allison, *Facts for Features*.
[2] The Weather Channel, *Cone of Uncertainty*.
[3] CNN, *Coverage of Mayor Nagin*.
[4] CNN, *Coverage of Mayor Nagin*.
[5] Burnett, John, *At a Shelter of Last Resort*.
[6] Burnett, John, *At a Shelter of Last Resort*

www.ingramcontent.com/pod-product-compliance
Lightning Source LLC
LaVergne TN
LVHW091549070526
838199LV00030B/616/J